Anne

from

Christopher.

X mas 1993.

GARDENING WITH

OLD
ROSES

GARDENING WITH
OLD
ROSES

ALAN SINCLAIR
&
ROSEMARY THODEY

CASSELL

We would like to thank the following people for their readily given assistance in preparing this book: Audrey Smithers, who gave Alan the necessary time, and Kate Upton, who did the same for Rosemary; Deb Cullinane for her help with the chapter on colour; and Donald Kerr, Librarian in the Rare Books Room at the Auckland City Library, for his assistance with the illustrations from *Curtis's Botanical Magazine*.

We are especially grateful to all those people who have allowed us to use photographs taken in their gardens: Dennis Greville, p. 39; Ruth Pettitt, 44, 149; David Steen, 49, 62, 130; Jan and Dennis Smith, 55, 83; Marnie Mackesy, 60, 63, 134, 155 (right); Jane Terpstra, 65, 92; Toni Sylvester, 67, 74, 97, 131, 133 (top), 146; Kay Jacobs, 79, 84, 109, 143; Liz Morrow, 86, 103, 104, 135 (right), 151, 155 (left); Liz and Geoff Brunsden, 94, 133 (bottom), 154, 157; Susanna Grace, 99; Rosemary Worley, 100, 147, 155; Vanessa Collinson, 102; Maree Forde-Harris, 105; Monica and Malcolm Drummond, 106; Tricia McKinnon, 135 (left), 156; Brett Schneideman, 137, 142; Jennie Bode, 144; Suzanne Turley, 148, 152; Barbara Toogood, 153. Photographs on pp. 43, 66, 68, 77, 78, 80, 98, 114, 126 and 127 were taken at Roseneath.

We would also like to thank Gil Hanly for the photographs on pp. 102 and 104, and Julian Matthews, editor of the *New Zealand Gardener*, and the magazine's publishers, Independent News Limited, for permission to include several photographs that have appeared in their magazine.

Cassell Publishers Limited
Villiers House, 41/47 Strand
London WC2N 5JE

First published in Great Britain 1993 by arrangement with
Godwit Press Limited, Auckland, New Zealand

British Library Cataloguing in Publication Data
A catalogue record for this book is available from the
British Library
ISBN 0-304-343544
Printed in Hong Kong

Front cover and title page: *R. x dupontii*, thought to be a cross between *R. gallica* and *R. moschata*, the Musk Rose, has beautiful large single blooms with a faint pink tinge and strong fine foliage. It is named after Monsieur Dupont, who had been the Empress Josephine's head gardener at Malmaison and was later Director of the Luxembourg Gardens in Paris.

Back cover: 'Wedding Day' with 'François Juranville' in the background.

Part I: *R. moyesii* seedling; Part II: 'Schneezwerg', an attractive Rugosa with pronounced stamens and beautifully formed flowers; Part III: 'Nancy Steen', a modern rose named after New Zealand's foremost authority on old roses, has flowers of wonderfully subtle colouring; Part IV: the cherry-red hips of the Rugosa Rose 'Typica'.

Chapter 1: Hand-coloured engravings and lithographs from *Curtis's Botanical Magazine; or Flower-garden displayed* (courtesy Auckland Public Library except *R. banksiae lutescens*, courtesy Auckland Museum).

Contents

Introduction

Most books currently available on old roses describe their subject in a dictionary or encyclopedic format arranged according to types or families within the genus *Rosa*. In our experience, we have found that people are constantly wanting to know what rose to grow where or which rose would be suitable for a particular purpose or position in the garden. Usually, this information is added in a brief appendix or can only be found by wading through the entire work. If you want a yellow rose to grow on a pillar, for example, which ones would be best; if you have a shady spot or want to grow a rose through a tree, what varieties will rise to the occasion; or what will smell wonderful by an entrance gate through which visitors must pass? These are the questions most often asked. In this book we have set about answering them in a readable and informative manner.

Alan Sinclair, who with his partner, Theo Verryt, has been growing roses for twenty-five years and now owns Roseneath, a rambling country garden and nursery specialising in old roses, has written Parts II and IV. Part II contains detailed and practical information on what rose to plant where, including descriptions of growth habits and the size mature plants can be expected to reach. Alan is used to answering precisely these questions on a daily basis as customers want to know what would be suitable for a rose hedge or what might be best to disguise an old shed, or what will cope with a shady woodland area or look good near water. A list of other roses suitable for each purpose has been included at the end of each chapter. For Part IV, covering the practical aspects of planting, pruning, spraying and general care of roses throughout the year, season by season, Alan has enlisted Theo's help as this is his particular area of expertise.

Some roses have been mentioned more than once because their various attributes render them suitable for more than one purpose. Roses like 'Jacques Cartier' and 'Comte de Chambord', for example, are excellent choices for the small garden and also make good hedges. 'Ispahan' could never be left out of a chapter on perfume and is equally indispensable for the large garden and the collector's garden. This merely serves to highlight once again the many attributes and virtues of these ancient symbols of state and church, literature, art and design, throughout the world and down through the ages.

R. bracteata

Rosemary Thodey has written Parts I and III dealing with the history and classification of old roses, and ideas for using them in the garden with an eye for colour and suitable companion plants. In writing articles for the *New Zealand Gardener*, Rosemary visits many gardens, and these particular aspects of landscape design have long been her special interest.

We hope this book will be of use and interest to the inexperienced as well as the more seasoned gardener. A list of over 500 roses has been included as an appendix for easy reference, giving a brief description including type, colour, perfume, flowering habits and the date it was introduced. From this the reader can refer to the index and find more detailed information in the relevant sections of the book. Although most of the roses listed are covered in detail in the text, it was not possible to include them all in a book of manageable proportions.

By adopting this fresh approach to the subject, we hope to show just how useful, versatile and adaptable the older varieties of rose, as well as some of the more recent hybrids which share their subtlety of shape and colour, can be: their inherent beauty and desirability has never been in question.

PART I

HISTORY
&
CLASSIFICATION

A brief history

However you enter the world of old roses, it won't be long before you are drawn into their romantic and fascinating history. At first it might seem a bit bewildering, but once you've succumbed to their fatal attraction, there is no going back. Part of the fascination is the way the history of roses stretches back through the centuries to ancient civilisations and what they have meant to generations of people. So let's go back to the beginning and see how the story unfolds.

The rose as we know it is part of the botanical family *Rosaceae*, which includes brambles and raspberries, strawberries and crab apples, hawthorns, rowans and wild cherries, some of the geums and alchemillas or lady's mantle, to say nothing of apricots, almonds, peaches, pears and the humble orchard apple. Many of these plants have similar flowers or blossom, with five petals each, and fruit just like the hips which follow the roses and are such a valuable source of vitamin C. All these similarities lead to the possibility of a single common ancestor. If so, it must be ancient beyond our imaginings because geologists tell us from the evidence provided by fossils that roses have been in existence for at least thirty-five million years.

From there we leap through the ages to some 4000 years ago, when Minoan goldsmiths made gold pins with single roses on the end. These were discovered in the Mochlos tombs on the island of Crete. Somewhere around that time an unknown artist included a rose in a fresco painted on a wall at Knossos, also in Crete. Discovered in the 1920s and identified as the Holy Rose, *Rosa sancta*, now known as *R.* x *richardii*, this early painting depicted a single pale pink bloom not unlike the exquisite creamy white *R.* x *dupontii*. It seems that this rose was also widely grown around the eastern end of the Mediterranean and that it was taken in the fourth century by Saint Frumentius from Phoenicia (now Syria) to Abyssinia (now Ethiopia), where it may still be found in the vicinity of churches. It has also been found in Egyptian tombs. As *R.* x *richardii* is thought to be a Gallica hybrid, its parent, *R. gallica*, must already have been in existence for some time and is believed to

R. gallica versicolor, 'Rosa Mundi'

be exceedingly ancient. It may have been brought to Italy and France by the Persians, who had known it since at least the twelfth century B.C.

R. gallica, or the Red Rose, *R. rubra*, is the common ancestor of many of our modern roses and a form of it became known as the Apothecary's Rose when physicians discovered that the petals kept their perfume when dried and that it was a useful astringent. Later, this variety, *R. gallica officinalis*, became known as the Rose of Provins, when it was adopted by the French who founded a thriving industry at Provins based on various conserves made from its dried petals. This was also the Red Rose of Lancaster which gave rise to the striped 'Rosa Mundi', named after the Fair Rosamund, Henry II's mistress.

Turning to ancient literature for evidence, we find that the Greek poet Homer, writing in about 700 B.C., mentions the rose in both *The Iliad* and *The Odyssey*: in *The Iliad* Aphrodite perfumes the dead Hector with rose oil, and in *The Odyssey* a passage begins, 'As soon as Dawn, with her rose-tinted hands had lit the East . . .' Edward A. Bunyard, in his book *Old Garden Roses*, points out that we cannot conclude from these references that the rose was grown in Greece but it was obviously known. In a meticulous search through Greek literature, the first real evidence Bunyard could find was a poem from

11

R. hispida (pimpinellifolia)   *R. multiflora carnea*

the fifth century B.C. by Anacreon, praising the rose for all those attributes we now automatically associate with this flower. 'It appears as the emblem of spring, the child of Venus, the companion of Bacchus, an apt comparison for maidenly blushes, as a medicine, and a scent.' We can see that the rose is already steeped in mythology, for the Greeks always sought a godly source for any special plant. So this poem talks about the birth of the rose coinciding with the birth of Venus, made immortal by Botticelli's painting depicting Venus rising from the sea in a shower of roses. Interestingly, the poem also talks about the 'various colours' of the rose, and there are many variations on the story about how it came to be red and pink as well as white. The tears or the blood of the gods, frequently Venus and Adonis, are traditionally the source of these magical events. It should not be forgotten that Venus was the goddess of beauty and the mother of love, a fitting source for the rose as symbol of beauty and romance.

Herodotus, 'the father of history', writing in about 445 B.C., speaks of double roses growing in the gardens of Midas, 'each one having sixty leaves (petals) and surpassing all other known roses in fragrance'. This is thought to have been the Damask Rose, *R. damascena*, again descended from *R. gallica*. Theophrastus (372–287 B.C.), 'the father of botany', who studied under Plato and then Aristotle, displays detailed knowledge of the cultivation of roses in his writings. He describes them as usually having five petals, sometimes twenty and occasionally a hundred. Further, he notes that flowers are produced more quickly when they are grown from cuttings than from seed and he even points out that they will have better flowers if they are 'cut over' or pruned.

From Greece we move to Rome, where the fortunes of the rose mirrored the rise and fall of that great empire. In the beginning the rose was used as an ornament at dinner when Roman life was still orderly and controlled. Before long, however, these simple rose crowns had become extravagant floods of flowers floating down from above and effectively burying the diners. Obviously a great number were grown to provide this sort of lavish spectacle, and there must have been an extraordinary boom in the gardening industry to keep up the supply. We know that the Romans were skilled engineers, and both Seneca (6 B.C.–A.D. 65) and Pliny the Elder (whose scientific curiosity led to his death at the hands of Vesuvius in A.D. 79) refer to the use of hothouses heated with tubes of warm water to make the roses bloom out of season. The poet Martial (ca. A.D. 40–102) refers to the fact that 'roses in winter bear the highest price', and it seems that the Autumn Damask Rose was grown in Egypt and transported to Rome to maintain the supply during the winter. This same rose, a cross between *R. gallica* and *R. moschata*, was mentioned by Virgil (ca. 70–19 B.C.) as the twice-flowering rose of Paestum. It was also found in frescoes at Pompeii. We hear of Nero spending unbelievable sums on roses for his banquets, of guests being suffocated by the overpowering scent of roses, and thick carpets of rose petals being laid for the important people of the moment. The curious phrase 'sub rosa' comes to us from the Romans, who would use a rose as a symbol of secrecy when meetings were held, whose contents were not to be divulged.

The roses known to the Greeks and Romans appear to have been produced from four species: *R. gallica*, *R. moschata*, and two roses from the Mediterranean area, *R. phoenicia* and *R. canina*.

Just as the Greeks and Romans had taken the rose to the farthest reaches of their empires, the Arabs carried it to new places as Islam spread east and west following the conquest of Persia in the seventh century. From Syria, where the invading Arabs succumbed to its spell, the rose found new homes in Spain to the west and India in the east. It is often depicted in Persian art, on tiles and porcelain and woven into tapestries and carpets, including stylised versions of the famous double yellow *R. hemisphaerica*, the Sulphur Rose.

In the Middle Ages the rose gradually emerged from disfavour as it became associated less with the excesses of earlier civilisations and more with Christianity. It was cultivated for its medicinal properties in the gardens of monasteries throughout Europe, and before long it was elevated to become an emblem of Christianity and especially of the saints. Its five petals came to be associated with and to symbolise Christ's five wounds, and red roses were used to represent the blood of Christian martyrs. The rosary dates from the beginning of the thirteenth century when Saint Dominic invented this new form of prayer after a revelation from the Virgin Mary. Originally the rosary beads were made from dried rose petals mixed to a kind of paste and slowly hardened. We also find the rose worked into the exquisite borders of illuminated books of the period, and Pope Clement V's Golden Rose shows the symbolic significance attached to it by the fourteenth century. This Golden Rose, with its highly stylised, artificial beauty, is almost mythical, the product of an age in which the material world was seen as the reflection of God's kingdom, the perfect golden world of heaven. Before long the rose was to be seen in churches everywhere, represented in the form with which we are still familiar, as circular windows of stained glass.

Moving into the Renaissance in Italy, with its emphasis on scientific observation, the careful study of nature in order to extract the truth rather than acceptance of traditional beliefs, the rose is drawn into sharper focus. We find the rose everywhere in Renaissance art, especially in the work of Botticelli. One of the figures in his *Primavera* has a rose in her mouth, and I have already mentioned the shower of roses which heralds the birth of Venus from the sea foam. The rose, together with gardening, became popular in fifteenth- and sixteenth-century Italy as part of the rebirth of classical learning and the growing emphasis on nature. Just as the Romans had built their houses around a central garden or courtyard, the atrium, Italians living in the fifteenth and sixteenth centuries returned to this idea of using the garden as an extension of the house by creating garden rooms. Garden design and horticultural knowledge were further challenges in a society where people sought to educate themselves as completely as possible.

For a brief period Holland was foremost in the development of the rose. The Dutch were acknowledged masters of still-life painting, capturing nature's every detail with accuracy and skill. From these paintings, beginning with Jan Breughel at the end of the sixteenth century through to Jan Van Huysum at the end of the seventeenth, we can trace the emerging importance of the rose as Dutch breeders worked to introduce new, ever fuller and more colourful varieties of the Cabbage Rose or *R. centifolia*, the rose of the painters. Once thought to have been one of the most ancient of roses, we now know, thanks to Dr Hurst's research, recorded in Graham Stuart Thomas's book *The Old Shrub Roses*, that this rose is of complex parentage and probably first appeared as a natural garden hybrid.

From Holland we turn to France, where Josephine Beauharnais awaits us. She married Napoleon in 1796 and set to work establishing her famous collection of roses at Malmaison near Paris. As Empress of France she was able to indulge her passion, adding more exotic varieties and importing both plants and gardeners, particularly from England. Even though France and England were at war, ships carrying new specimens were granted safe passage and many plants were also shipped back to Malmaison from countries conquered by Napoleon's armies.

Perhaps Josephine's greatest contribution lay in her encouragement of the breeding of new roses. Any garden containing old roses will have some with French names, harking back to this brilliant era when the French were firmly at the forefront of rose breeding. By commissioning Redouté to paint the roses growing at Malmaison, more than two hundred varieties, Josephine made a further great contribution to art as well as horticulture. These popular works, executed in the midst of turmoil and first published in a series of folios between 1802 and 1816, serve to keep alive an image of the tranquil beauty which Josephine must have enjoyed and which we can still enjoy today.

And so to England, to Chaucer, Spenser and Shakespeare, and all the other writers who have used the rose again and again as an image of beauty and love. Nicholas Hilliard's famous miniature portrait (about 1590) of a young nobleman leaning against a tree, hand on heart, surrounded by wild roses, conjures up perfectly the gentle, romantic, courtly role the rose was to play throughout this period of history. Earlier, though, its role in England had not been so peaceful or pleasant. The Romans brought roses to England during their occupation, and later the Crusaders were probably responsible for bringing home many different forms from the East during the eleventh, twelfth and thirteenth centuries. The rose soon became well established as a royal emblem, having first been adopted by Edward I towards the end of the thirteenth century. During the Wars of the Roses, 1455–1485, the House of

R. muscosa

R. arvensis, the Field Rose

York took the White Rose of England, probably *R. x alba*, a descendant of the Damask Rose and the native Dog Rose, *R. canina*, for its emblem, while the House of Lancaster had used the red rose *R. gallica officinalis* since the time of Henry IV. Shakespeare begins his play *Henry VI* with the Lancastrians picking red roses and the Yorkists white, in support of the Earl of Somerset on the one hand and Richard Plantagenet on the other. Peace was not restored until thirty years later, when the marriage of Henry Tudor and Elizabeth of York re-united the two sides and established the House of Tudor. The red and white Tudor Rose 'York and Lancaster', or *R. x damascena versicolor*, was then adopted as the royal emblem and is still used today.

In 1596 Gerard produced the first catalogue of roses, some sixteen in all, growing in his garden at Holborn. His writings are significant in that they show that by this time in Elizabethan England the rose had moved from the vegetable patch into the flower garden, in recognition of its beauty and fragrance rather than its herbal or medicinal uses. Shakespeare was writing nearby at this time, and his numerous references to roses — the Damask, Sweet Musk, Eglantine and many others — serve not only to cement the powerful imagery of the rose in literature but must also reflect its growing stature.

It is time to turn to China and discover the remarkable events which were to revolutionise the breeding of roses and lead to the modern forms we know today. The Chinese have gardened forever, and China is the home of many of our most familiar roses like the Chinas, the Teas, the Rugosas, Polyanthas and Banksias. Silk screens dating from the tenth century clearly depict roses, but it was not until the eighteenth century that these Chinese roses were introduced to Europe. The revolutionary characteristic they brought with them was, of course, their capacity for perpetual flowering. Once this miraculous gene was bred into the European roses, the possibilities were endless. Four roses, which became known as the four stud Chinas, were chiefly responsible for this revolution at the hands of the European rose breeders. 'Slater's Crimson China' was brought to England in 1792, 'Parsons' Pink China' in 1793, 'Hume's Blush Tea-scented China' in 1810, and 'Parks' Yellow Tea-scented China' in 1824. From these were to come the Portlands, Noisettes, Bourbons, Hybrid Perpetuals, the less-hardy Teas and Hybrid Teas and, via the Polyanthas, the cluster-flowered or Floribunda Roses.

What of North America, which had several of its own native roses to begin with? So popular is the rose there today that it is the adopted flower of several states. *R. laevigata*, for example, is known as the Cherokee Rose. Its Chinese origins long since forgotten, it has become a part of the landscape since it arrived there towards the end of the eighteenth century. There are at least two different versions of the story of how it came to be known as the Cherokee Rose. In one, an Indian girl is turned into a flower with particularly savage thorns to save her from a warring tribe; in another, women and girls from the Cherokee tribe used to braid the flowers into their hair. During the

R. lutea, R. foetida, Austrian Briar   *R. semperflorens*, 'Slater's Crimson China'

last century the Americans have played their part in breeding many of today's stalwarts, especially the Wichuraiana Ramblers like 'Dorothy Perkins' and 'New Dawn' as well as many Floribundas.

The rose is not native to any land south of the equator, but just as it had spread to new countries with the expansion of ancient empires, so it was to be carried south as South Africa, Australia and New Zealand were colonised. As we have seen with North America, all of these countries provided such rich breeding grounds that they, in their turn, each added substantially to the burgeoning world of the genus *Rosa*.

Roses had been introduced to Australia by the end of the eighteenth century and were often used on fences around the settlers' cottages as well as within their gardens. The old China Roses soon gained in popularity when they were brought out from England because of their long-flowering habit, and early lists include the white Moss, 'Quatre Saisons Blanc Mousseux', and the Sweet Briar so often mentioned in early New Zealand records. The number of roses in the colony quickly increased, shadowing their development in England, where the popular new Hybrid Perpetuals soon gained centre stage in the nineteenth century. In the first half of this century Australian rose breeding was given a great boost by Alister Clark, who lived at 'Glenara' in Bulla near Melbourne. He sent two nurserymen the length and breadth of Europe to find all the Great Roses listed by William Robinson, whom he had met in England. Subsequently he used one of these,

17

R. gigantea, originally from Burma, to breed a new range of climbers better suited to the hot dry landscape of Australia.

In many cases the missionaries arrived in these 'new' lands long before organised groups of settlers, and this was undoubtedly how New Zealand gained its first roses. Ken Nobbs, co-founder with Toni Sylvester of Heritage Roses in New Zealand, tells us in an article on New Zealand's oldest roses that the first rose to reach these shores arrived on the brig 'Active' on Christmas Day 1814. On board was a party of the Church Missionary Society from England, led by the Reverend Samuel Marsden, which included four women, and it seems that 'one or more of these women cared for at least one rose on the journey and it was carried ashore with loving care along with the stores'. The missionaries settled at a place called Oihi, near Rangihoua Pa in the Bay of Islands, and the rose, *R. chinensis* var. *semperflorens* or 'Slater's Crimson China', was planted and grew. As Nancy Steen records, a border of this small rose was planted from cuttings of the Oihi rose in 1822, by Samuel Butler, in front of the newly built Kemp homestead at the head of the Kerikeri Inlet. Kemp House is now preserved as the oldest wooden house in New Zealand.

According to Mrs Steen, the Sweet Briar and Dog Rose were grown from seed, and hedges of these roses were well established in the north of New Zealand by 1830, the missionaries taking them with them wherever they moved. The Maoris called the Sweet Briar 'Te Mihanere', 'The Missionary'. But by 1900 the Sweet Briar had been declared a noxious weed as it had spread so vigorously.

In 1828 we have the first reference to a Cabbage or Centifolia Rose, when George Clarke recalls the death of his sister, aged three months, from whooping cough. His parents were missionaries and they were living briefly at Kemp House at the time. He says that his father had received, a short time before, 'a box of plants from Sydney, among them some precious cabbage roses, the first I suppose to be grown in New Zealand. I remember his taking me by the hand, nipping off a half opened bud and then walking into the study and his putting the flower in the dead baby's hand'. This incident was to come back to him 'with the sight and scent of cabbage roses and it is a sort of faint musk to my memory'.

Much further south, in 1840, the French settled at Akaroa on Banks Peninsula in the South Island, bringing with them some of the old Gallicas, Mosses, and Damasks, which are still cherished there today. Jessie Mould, in an article called 'Roses for a French Cottage Garden', tells us that 'in late October the hedges in Akaroa are a mass of pink and red China roses — Old Blush and Fabvier, probably, as there is sometimes a streak of white on the crimson petals. This crimson China is known by the older folk as Bishop Pompallier's Rose. He brought cuttings from the Bay of Islands, in the far north of New Zealand, when he visited his French flock at Akaroa.' Interestingly, the French used to roll cuttings in dry moss and pack them in metal surveyors' tubes to send them to the Southern Hemisphere.

The earliest rose catalogue unearthed by Nancy Steen was that put out by William Hale of Nelson in 1860. As she writes, 'the striking thing about Hale's Catalogue is that he introduced roses into this young and sparsely settled country within a few years of their being bred in Europe'. Despite the difficulties of sending roses so far in the early days of settlement, many must have survived because they were soon to be found the length and breadth of the country, flourishing around homesteads and in public gardens and cemeteries everywhere. Lady Barker, writing to her sister in England in 1865 (in *Station Life in New Zealand*) brings it to life for us: 'How I wish they could see this in England and not only see but *feel* it, for the very breath one draws on such a morning is happiness; the air is so light and balmy it seems to heal the lungs as you inhale it. The verandah is covered with honeysuckles and other creepers and the gable end of the house, where the bow window of the drawing room projects, is one mass of yellow Banksia roses in full blossom.'

R. banksiae lutescens

CHAPTER 2

A simple guide to all those types

WILD OR SPECIES ROSES

Wild or species roses are the parents of all the roses we grow today. The European species include Shakespeare's Eglantine, *R. eglanteria* or Sweet Briar; *R. canina* or the Dog Rose; *R. arvensis* or the Field Rose; *R. pimpinellifolia* (previously *spinosissima*) or the Scotch Rose; *R. villosa*, the Apple Rose or *R. pomifera*; and there are several American natives: *R. virginiana*, *R. carolina*, *R. nitida* and *R. foliolosa*, among others. From Asia or the East we have the China Rose (*R. chinensis*), *R. multiflora*, ancestor of today's cluster-flowered rose, the Banksias and the Rugosas, while the Middle East gave rise to the only yellow roses, also of the *pimpinellifolia* family or subgenus. The single *R. foetida* or *R. lutea*, the Austrian Briar, was known in England by 1597, and the double *R. hemisphaerica*, the Sulphur Rose, was introduced to Europe in about 1600 but didn't like the climate, was difficult to propagate and turned out to be sterile as well. Breeders had to wait another 200 years before the arrival of another double yellow rose, *R. foetida persiana*, the Persian Yellow, before they could begin to develop the many different yellows which are so commonplace today. The real breakthrough came in 1900 when Pernet-Ducher produced 'Soleil d'Or' from the Persian Yellow.

Those who are smitten with old roses often end up deeply enamoured of the species roses, those self-sufficient, simple beauties that have survived the centuries. They are almost all single flowers with five petals (*R. sericea* being the only species with four), blooming for a few brief weeks, their delicate fragrant flowers followed by glowing hips, all amid generous foliage. *R. chinensis* has a weighty role in that it was recurrent or repeat-flowering and was therefore leapt upon by rose breeders in Europe when it arrived from China early in the eighteenth century.

Interestingly, some of the roses which are closest to these originals are

20

R. pimpinellifolia altaica, a parent of the Frühlings roses (left) and 'Abbotswood' (right)

also some of the most enduring in the highly fickle world of rose fashion. 'Stanwell Perpetual', for example, a Scotch Rose brought out in 1838, is still very much with us despite its delicate powder-puff appearance, with its pale pink fully double blooms and fine foliage. Kordes of Germany has more recently given us the 'Frühlings' (Spring) series of roses, and Roy Shepherd's 'Golden Wings' also comes from the Scotch stable. Or there is the superb 'Fritz Nobis', descendant of the Sweet Briar, or the delightful 'Abbotswood', offspring of the Dog Rose, *R. canina*.

From these ancient masterpieces, then, come the myriad garden varieties devotees chatter so knowledgeably about on garden tours and the like. As we look at each group, we'll illustrate their main characteristics by picking out a few typical representatives. Soon you too will be able to throw in a Damask or Bourbon, Alba or Centifolia, with supreme nonchalance.

GALLICAS

Gallicas are low-growing, spreading shrubs which sucker easily and tolerate poor soils. Their leaves are a dull green and the hips are insignificant, but the flowers are relatively large and held erect, appearing early in the season in late spring. The original *R. gallica* or *R. rubra* (the Red Rose) was well known to the Greeks and Romans and has been prized for its medicinal uses since ancient times. It was adopted by the House of Lancaster after Edmund, Earl of Lancaster, took it as his emblem on his return to England in 1277 after avenging the death of a mayor of Provins as requested by the King of France.

'Anaïs Ségales'   'Tuscany Superb'

My favourite Gallica is 'Anaïs Ségales', with its smoky purple flowers opening out flat to reveal an appealing green eye in the centre. It is one of those roses which changes colour as it opens, from a rosy purple through to a lilac-pink before finally fading to a delicate blue-grey shade. Much of the attraction of old roses lies in these subtle developments, along with the wonderful fragrance. 'Anaïs Ségales' is typical of the Gallica or French Roses, with its low-growing habit and flat perfectly formed flowers. Even its colour complexities almost cover the range for the Gallicas as they come in pinks (no whites) variously tinged with blue to create mauves and lilacs through to deep rich burgundy-maroons and purples. It is very easy to grow and suckers freely, which is why it is often found in old cemeteries and abandoned sites, where it has been left to romp.

Other popular roses in this group are 'Rosa Mundi', the striped rose; the rich velvety 'Tuscany Superb', deep burgundy in colour; 'Charles de Mills', another rich plum-coloured variety; and 'Cardinal de Richelieu', a purplish maroon. Two delightful soft pink Gallicas are 'Belle Isis' and 'Duchesse de Montebello'. 'Complicata' is a single Gallica which is large enough to be classed as a climber but can be grown as a useful big shrub at the back of a border. The flowers are pink with a paler centre warmed by attractive golden stamens.

DAMASKS

The Damasks are shrouded in mystery. It is thought that the name came from a link with Damascus in Syria and that it was probably brought back to Europe by the Crusaders. Damasks are mentioned by Greek and Roman writers, both the Summer Damask, *R. damascena*, and the Autumn Damask, *R.* x *damascena semperflorens* or *R.* x *bifera*. The latter repeats in autumn and is known in France as the Quatre Saisons Rose and in Spain as the Alexandria Rose, indicating that it probably arrived there from Egypt. Both the Summer and the Autumn Damask are descended from *R. gallica*, but the former has *R. phoenicia* as its other parent whereas the latter has *R. moschata*. Their mixed ancestry makes them difficult to define, but they do grow taller than the Gallicas and their flowers nod on pliant shoots arching from the centre of the plants. They have a delicious and distinctive fragrance from which attar of roses is made in the East.

One look at the beautiful 'Mme Hardy' and it is likely that you will find, if not manufacture, a space for this gentle Damask somewhere in the back of a border. Some would say, and I would be one of them, that 'Mme Hardy' is the most beautiful white rose in existence. The flower is similar in shape to that of 'Anaïs Ségales', being full and flat with a green eye, the whole creating an impression of incredible perfection.

Other desirable Damasks include the unusual and possibly very ancient 'Hebe's Lip', of unique charm with its milky white, open flowers tipped with

'Ispahan'

red, and 'Ispahan', a warm pink, free-flowering and long-blooming variety conjuring up the romance of ancient Persia. A modern variety is the clear pink 'St Nicholas', discovered as a seedling in Yorkshire in 1950.

ALBAS

Another ancient group, the Albas, emerged as a cross between *R. damascena* and *R. canina*. They have distinctive and very attractive grey-green foliage, flower in early summer in shades from white to pink, and are worth trying in difficult places in shade or where tree roots invade mercilessly.

The delightfully scented Albas are an integral part of British history. As we have seen, *R.* x *alba* itself was probably the emblem of the House of York during the Wars of the Roses, and the great double white form, 'Maxima', is also known as the Jacobite Rose or Bonnie Prince Charlie's Rose. It seems likely that this was the painters' rose of the Renaissance. Another white semi-double form thought by some to have been the White Rose of York is 'Semi-plena'.

'Celestial' is an exquisitely simple soft pink rose, which definitely performs better in light or dappled shade. 'Königin von Dänemark' or 'Queen of Denmark' is another pink Alba, with a more formal shape to its flowers, and the smaller 'Félicité Parmentier' has even more perfectly formed reflexing blooms in a crisper icy pink.

CENTIFOLIAS

The Centifolias were originally thought to be exceedingly ancient because of references to hundred-petalled roses by Greek writers like Theophrastus

'Celestial'

'Hebe's Lip'

'Fantin-Latour'

(372–287 B.C.). Scientific analysis has revealed, however, that they are of complex lineage and probably occurred by chance and were then developed and refined by Dutch breeders in the seventeenth century.

The incomparable 'Fantin-Latour' is one of the better-known Centifolia (hundred-petalled) or Cabbage Roses, so called because of the way the numerous petals curve inwards, hiding the centre. It is a tall arching rose with clear pink flowers deepening in colour in the centre and can be grown as a small climber with support. This is the best way to see its richly perfumed flowers, which tend to hang downwards. Having seen it, you will know why another name the Centifolias have earned is 'the rose of the painters'; they occur again and again in Dutch and Flemish still-life painting of the

'William Lobb'

'Old Blush China'

seventeenth and eighteenth centuries. 'Fantin-Latour' itself is named after a French flower painter who lived from 1836 to 1904. Centifolia has also been called the Holland or Province Rose and nowadays the Rose of Provence. 'Juno' is a paler pink version, and 'Rose de Meaux' is a smaller-growing form with clear pink flowers.

MOSS ROSES

These roses first appeared in Holland early in the eighteenth century. They are sports or mutations from the Centifolias and look much the same except that the green sepals covering the buds are 'mossy'. If you touch the moss it feels sticky and leaves its scent on your fingers. The Victorians loved them as a novelty, and today they remind us of that era of overcrowded rooms, evoking a sense of pampered comfort. 'Mme Louis Lévêque', one of the best known, has full pink blooms. 'William Lobb' or 'Old Velvet Moss' is another, with very rich deep purple-crimson flowers that fade to lavender as they age. It's a superbly dressed rose because the effect is exactly that of a soft, luxurious garment made of old velvet, unfurling to give just a hint of the slightly lighter reverse of the petals when all is revealed.

CHINA ROSES

With the arrival of the first China Roses in Europe in the eighteenth century, the modern rose was effectively born. The ancient European roses had, by and large, only one flowering season, but by crossing them with the per-petual-flowering China Roses, new varieties with this desirable trait were soon developed. The first two China Roses of importance to be introduced were 'Slater's Crimson China' or *R. indica* (later corrected to *chinensis* to show that it came from China, not India) *semperflorens* in 1792 and 'Parsons' Pink China' or 'Old Blush China' in 1793. For 'Old Blush China' it was a second introduction as it had been brought to Sweden from Canton by Peter Osbeck in 1752 and from there to England by 1769, though its potential had remained untapped.

'Old Blush China' has a special place in my affections as it was one of the first old roses to reawaken me to the simple charms of the older varieties. 'Mutabilis' is another desirable China Rose. Nearly always in flower, it is sometimes known as the Butterfly Rose because of the almost fluttering effect of its single flowers, which range in colour from yellow through a coppery pink to crimson. An attractive feature of the Chinas which was passed on to the Bourbons is their characteristic of deepening in colour instead of becoming paler and washed-out looking as the flowers age.

The Chinas include many of the tiny miniature roses which are indispensable where space is at a premium. 'Anna Maria de Montravel' and 'Little White Pet', a dwarf form of 'Félicité et Perpétue', cover themselves densely

'Comte de Chambord'

with the smallest of double white flowers, the latter opening from pink buds. 'Cécile Brunner' or the Sweetheart Rose is universally loved, with its tiny pink buds opening to pale pink. Sometimes classed as a Hybrid Tea, it is more often found among the Chinas these days. 'Bloomfield Abundance' is exactly the same but has longer sepals extending beyond the buds. A soft apricot version is to be found in the exquisite 'Perle d'Or'. From a union brought about by Ann Bentall (one of the Reverend Pemberton's gardeners) between the Dwarf Pompom 'Paul Crampel' and 'Lady Gay' in 1932 came that very familiar 'The Fairy', which seems to flower forever.

A remarkable curiosity, thought to have been around for more than a century, is the Green Rose or *R. viridiflora*, literally a mixture of green and brown. It can be an acquired taste but it looks great with other flowers in floral arrangements.

PORTLAND ROSES

The Portland Roses, said to have originated in Italy but named after the Duchess of Portland in the latter part of the eighteenth century, are supposedly the product of a China Rose and a Gallica or Damask (or possibly a seedling of these two). The few remaining Portlands are useful for smaller gardens as they flower continuously and are not large plants. The two best known, which were bred in France in the 1860s, are 'Comte de Chambord' and 'Jacques Cartier'. The former is a strong pink fully double flower, lighter at the edges, while the latter is a lighter pink of similar shape.

BOURBONS

The Bourbons originated from the chance crossing of a China Rose with a Damask, planted together as hedges in 1817 on an island off the coast of Africa then called Île de Bourbon (now Réunion). The combination of a long flowering season from their China parent and the alluring scent gained from the Damasks resulted in some legendary roses, now firmly re-established as indispensable. Many of them have large, almost globular flowers, bursting with fine petals which unfurl to reveal perfect form.

'Souvenir de la Malmaison', for example, is exquisitely formed, fully quartered, with the softest blush-pink blooms which just keep coming. It is often found on the graves of babies and children in older cemeteries, and it is not hard to see why it was chosen. In 1950 'Souvenir de St Anne's' appeared as a sport of 'Souvenir de la Malmaison' and a worthy one at that. Of the same soft pink, it is only semi-double in form, which gives it decided appeal, as well as making it far less inclined to succumb to wet weather.

The cupped pink 'La Reine Victoria' and its sport 'Mme Pierre Oger' are two other popular roses in this group. The latter has particularly attractive colouring, its creamy, shell-like, almost translucent petals blushed pink at the edges and becoming deeper in intense sunlight. 'Louise Odier' is a perfectly formed clear pink rose, almost too good to be true, while 'Mme Isaac Pereire' has the distinction of being considered the most fragrant rose of all. It can also boast amazing formation, the petals swelling up into a precise quartered arrangement of rich fuchsia-maroon. 'Mme Ernst Calvat' is its pale pink

'Souvenir de la Malmaison'

'Souvenir de St Anne's'

sport, also blessed with a ripe-raspberry fragrance.

Several of the fascinating striped roses are Bourbons; perhaps the most arresting of all is that highly voluptuous fragrant rose 'Variegata di Bologna', which stands head and shoulders above the crowd with its delectable milk-and-cherry-plum colouring.

HYBRID PERPETUALS

Hybrid Perpetuals came from crosses between Bourbons and many other 'perpetual' varieties such as Portlands and Chinas early in the nineteenth century. They are sometimes thought to be rather large, coarse roses, but there is something comforting and nostalgic about their image of Victorian opulence. If you peg down the long shoots these roses put out, they will flower all along the length. Colours range from white through the pinks to dark red and purple.

'Frau Karl Druschki' is the best-known white, undeniably handsome but unfortunately completely lacking in scent. 'Mrs John Laing' has also stood the test of time, with its attractive silver-pink double blooms which are very fragrant. Of particular charm is the much rarer 'Souvenir du Docteur Jamain', rescued from obscurity by Vita Sackville-West, who discovered it growing in an old nursery. A 'sweetly and sentimentally scented' deep wine-red, it demands a little protection from the sun; as only she could put it, 'he burns'.

TEA ROSES

Tea Roses also originated in China, probably from a chance crossing of the China Rose, *R. chinensis*, with *R. gigantea*, a vigorous climbing rose. Unfortunately, they are not well suited to the colder climate of northern Europe, where they are often grown under glass, but they thrive in New Zealand, Australia, the warmer parts of America, South Africa and the Mediterranean.

'Jean Ducher' is a popular Tea Rose which produces its graceful, soft blooms of palest buff to creamy coral-pink almost continuously. Others include the coppery red 'Général Schablikine', and 'Archiduc Joseph' (known in New Zealand as 'Monsieur Tillier'), creamy white 'Devoniensis', and the beautiful pink 'Duchesse de Brabant'. This group includes some highly desirable climbers, which are covered in chapter 3.

HYBRID TEAS

The first Hybrid Tea is generally accepted to be 'La France', introduced by Guillot in France in 1867. It was soon followed by another fine pink rose, 'Lady Mary Fitzwilliam', bred by Bennett in England. The new race of Hybrid Teas resulted from crossing the Teas with the Hybrid Perpetuals, thereby combining the high-centred shape, fine leaves and desirable colours

'Souvenir du Docteur Jamain'

'Frau Karl Druschki'

'Archiduc Joseph'

31

'Blanc Double de Coubert'　　　　　　　　'Roseraie de l'Hay'

R. rugosa 'Typica'

32

of the Teas with the hardiness, strong flower-stems and the more vigorous growth habit of the Hybrid Perpetuals. As the yellows of the roses raised by Pernet-Ducher were introduced into the new breed, they went from strength to strength, culminating, perhaps, in that great rose 'Peace', a universal symbol of hope at the end of the Second World War.

FLORIBUNDAS

Floribundas were developed from the small Polyantha Roses, which had inherited their clusters of flowers from *R. multiflora*, a Japanese rambler, and their perpetual-flowering habit from their other parent, probably a China Rose. During the 1920s a Danish breeder called Svend Poulsen crossed the Dwarf Polyanthas with Hybrid Teas to create a new type of rose called Hybrid Polyanthas. Over time these roses were developed further until by the 1950s they had become known as Floribundas. Nowadays they are sometimes referred to as 'cluster-flowered' to distinguish them from the Hybrid Teas or 'large-flowered' roses. In America the taller-growing Floribundas like 'Queen Elizabeth' are known as Grandifloras.

RUGOSAS

Known as the Rose of Japan, *R. rugosa* is also found in the wild in northern China, Korea and eastern Siberia, and is easily recognised by its distinctive, heavily veined leaves, quite apart from the singular beauty of its flowers. These are incredibly tough, compact shrubs often recommended for seaside sites as they withstand the elements and don't need or like a lot of fussing. Most of the Rugosas bear large, glossy hips, like plump little apples of unbelievable perfection, often borne concurrently with the flowers. Many of the hybrids common today were bred around the turn of the century and are now becoming increasingly popular as hedging plants, for which they are most effective.

Many have large single, rather fragile-looking flowers, such as the arrestingly beautiful 'Frau Dagmar Hastrup', which has light pink flowers — once seen, never forgotten. *R. rugosa alba* has the same open, innocent appearance in the form of large single white flowers. 'Calocarpa' dates from 1891 and has distinctive violet-crimson single flowers. The biggest single flowers of all are to be found on 'Scabrosa', with its huge saucers of fuchsia-pink petals which give way to equally large red hips. *R. rugosa* 'Typica' has mauve-pink blooms with rosy red hips as well.

Some superb double white Rugosas are available, like the gentle 'Blanc Double de Coubert', fresh snow-white with a fragile texture and generous fragrance. The offspring of *R. rugosa* and 'Sombreuil', it was bred in France in a village called Coubert in 1892. 'Mme Georges Bruant' is an earlier (1887) product of the same parents, with pearlier white loosely double blooms of considerable tea charm. 'Schneezwerg' is another double white with medium

'Penelope'

flowers, produced continuously, so that the later combination of hips and blooms is an attractive sight. The hardy modern hybrid 'Henry Hudson' deserves mention here, with its enchantingly fresh white blooms tinted pink.

'Hansa' is a loosely double magenta, while 'Roseraie de l'Häy' is a deeper colour with more of a purple toning to its smaller blooms. 'Charles Albanel', a vigorous ground-cover rose, is a modern hybrid with cerise-red blooms. 'Sarah van Fleet' is a much softer pink, reputedly a good hedging plant, as are many of the Rugosas, with their dense shrubby manner of growth.

The Grootendorst Rugosas all have frilled edges like carnations; 'Pink Grootendorst' is probably the most widely grown, with its delightfully different little pink flowers in clusters. 'Fimbriata' is not of this family but has similar serrated petals of white blushed pink.

Yellow is a rare colour among the Rugosas, making the soft buff-yellow blooms of 'Agnes' even more appealing.

HYBRID MUSKS

The Musk Roses we grow today are distant descendants of *R. moschata*, the Musk Rose, most of them bred by the Reverend J. Pemberton of Havering in Essex around the turn of the century. They are invariably healthy, strongly

'Cornelia'

growing, highly fragrant roses which flower prolifically. Not strictly speaking old roses, they belong here by virtue of their subtle shades and gentler shape. In warmer climates they frequently take on the dimensions of small climbers and are often treated as such.

'Penelope', for example, a favourite of Vita Sackville-West, is a soft cream with deeper warm peach tones, the colour of the buds before they open. 'Felicia' is another popular Hybrid Musk in apricot-salmon-pink, and 'Cornelia' has smaller flattish double coral-pink flowers which just keep coming. 'Ballerina', a chance seedling nurtured by Ann Bentall, one of Joseph Pemberton's gardeners, who carried on breeding new roses with her husband, John, after Pemberton's death, has big sprays of tiny pink and white flowers. The more recent 'Lavender Lassie', bred by Kordes in 1959, always looks attractive with its clusters of lilac-pink flowers.

'Buff Beauty', another of Ann Bentall's creations, is aptly named, with its generous supply of dull yellow-gold blooms. 'Danaë' is a delightful clear yellow which becomes paler as the flowers age, as all the Hybrid Musks tend to do. 'Moonlight' is an ivory-white, lovely when glowing out of light dappled shade, whereas 'Prosperity' produces a great froth of pearly white double blooms.

In full flight, 'Wilhelm', with its clusters of deep red buds opening to sheer crimson flowers, is an equally arresting sight.

35

ENGLISH ROSES

In 1961 David Austin of Albrighton, near Wolverhampton in England, released his first New English Rose, 'Constance Spry'. Its parents were the Gallica 'Belle Isis' and a Floribunda called 'Dainty Maid'. By crossing one of the old roses with a modern Floribunda, he had succeeded in producing a captivating rose, one I am perfectly happy to wait for each spring when it smothers a wall of the house with its lovely full pink blooms which smell divine. Since then Austin has produced a whole range of roses which are similar in form to the old roses, mostly fragrant and having the added advantage of remontancy or repeat-flowering; in fact, some flower continuously. By using an old variety as one of the parents and a Hybrid Tea or Floribunda as the other, much of the simple yet refined formation which gives old roses their special charm is preserved. In warmer climates many of these English Roses grow tall enough to be classed as pillar roses or small climbers.

One of the most popular must be the superb buttercup-yellow 'Graham Thomas'; 'Yellow Charles Austin' is another success story; 'Charles Austin' itself is a buff or pale coppery yellow. 'English Garden' is more of a creamy primrose-yellow, double as can be, while 'Windrush' is a gentle, open semi-double of palest primrose.

'Heritage' is pure salmon-pink of perfect, slightly cupped form, and 'Abraham Darby' has a larger heavier head with peach and apricot overtones. 'The Reeve' is also rather cupped, very full and pure pink, a bit like a larger

'Charles Austin'

'Windrush'

'Graham Thomas'

37

'Constance Spry'

blowzier 'Raubritter'. 'Mary Rose' is here to stay, with its generous supply of endearing, slightly muddled, rosy pink blooms which gradually fade to pale pink. So too is 'Gertrude Jekyll', an enchanting rose with its deep pink centre lightening subtly towards the edges, and tightly packed petals reminiscent of its parent, the Portland Rose 'Comte de Chambord'. 'Dapple Dawn' is an attractive single pink with white centre.

'Red Coat' is pure scarlet with yellow stamens, semi-double, large-growing and flowering for ever. 'Prospero' is on a much smaller scale but has perfectly double quartered blooms, which change from deep rich magenta to dark purple. Of similar old-fashioned crimson-purple complexity is 'William Shakespeare'.

CHAPTER 3

Climbers and ramblers

Roses climbing and rambling over walls and fences, cascading from bowers, pergolas and walkways, and creating huge wild hedges along the roadside add a special dimension to the value of the genus as landscaping plants. Their place in large country gardens is obvious, but these days, when more and more people live in smaller and smaller spaces in large cities, growing them on walls and vertical supports can provide many more square metres of vertical display area to enhance that limited space.

In older parts of cities it's not uncommon to see walls smothered in old roses; even those which have clearly been left to their own devices and ignored for years usually add great charm to the dwelling behind the wall. In recent years many delightful old houses have been restored and it is wonderful to see that often their gardens have been replanted in keeping with that

R. multiflora seedling with *Orlaya grandiflora* in front

'Lamarque'

'Maréchal Niel'

'Crépuscule'

era, using old roses in abundance. Some of the tiniest gardens are full of old roses, and the owners have made good use of upright surfaces and structures, including perimeter walls, the walls of the house itself, pergolas and summer-houses, tripods, arches and standards to create an effect of colour flowing from rigid form.

It is generally accepted that climbers differ from ramblers in that they grow stiffly upright, eventually forming thick, woody trunks rather like trees, whereas ramblers arch out from the base with pliant, supple shoots that roam over the ground if left to themselves. However, these distinctions are becom-ing blurred as the genus *Rosa* becomes increasingly complicated and inter-twined, and breeders continue to try to blend the grace, charm and perfume of the old wild species or ramblers with the repeat-flowering habits of the larger-flowered, more interbred or hybridised climbers. A few of the ancient wild climbers, especially *R. moschata*, *R. gigantea*, *R. chinensis* and *R. multi-flora*, have been responsible for many of our current hybrids.

In warmer climates many shrub roses take on the proportions of climbers and can easily be trained to adorn a wall, pillar or fence even though they are not, strictly speaking, climbers. Occasionally a non-climbing rose will pro-duce, naturally and spontaneously, a different type of shoot, sometimes a climbing one; this is called a sport, and further plants can usually be propagated from it. In this way, climbing versions of many roses have arisen.

Climbers

NOISETTES

The Noisettes include such old classics as 'Lamarque' and 'Mme Alfred Carrière'. Their story begins in the garden of John Champneys, a rice farmer in Charleston, South Carolina, in the year 1802. From two plants growing in his garden at that time — the China Rose 'Old Blush China' and the climbing *R. moschata*, or the Musk Rose — John Champneys raised a seedling which was to become the well-known, once-flowering climbing rose 'Champneys' Pink Cluster'. Apparently, in one of those odd quirks of nature, if you cross a once-flowering rose with a repeat-flowering one, the offspring will be once-flowering but the second-generation plants are usually recurrent. Seeds of 'Champneys' Pink Cluster' were sown by a French nurseryman living in Charleston, Philippe Noisette, who sent the most promising of the resulting seedlings to his brother in Paris, Louis Noisette, another nurseryman. Thus began a group of roses loved the world over for the incredible generosity of their fragrant flowers, which are either perpetual or recurrent.

Early Noisettes include 'Autumnalis' and 'Aimée Vibert'. By 1830 breeders had crossed a newly imported yellow, tea-scented China Rose with

'Gracilis', an accommodating rosy pink Boursault

the early Noisettes, resulting in the Tea Noisettes. Colours range from yellow through to white, with the flowers usually forming a large cluster. Apart from the very floriferous lemony white 'Lamarque', already mentioned, and 'Mme Alfred Carrière', whose looser white flowers have a hint of pink occasionally, the group includes the yellow roses 'Céline Forestier' and the deeper 'Crépuscule', 'Alister Stella Gray', 'Cloth of Gold' and the tender but exquisite buttery yellow 'Maréchal Niel'.

CLIMBING TEAS

Gardeners in the warmer climates of the Southern Hemisphere are lucky to be able to grow the Climbing Teas so easily, because they are a special group captured perfectly by Graham Stuart Thomas, who wrote, 'I wish I had a large, slightly heated greenhouse to accommodate them. They are too good to lose forever; the gentle elegance of bygone days is preserved in them.'

In the northern part of New Zealand, for example, 'Souvenir de Mme Léonie Viennot' grows like a weed, ambling along many an old picket fence, with its yellow and coppery pink flowers emerging from strong pinky red buds full of the promise of that divine tea scent. 'Sombreuil' is a rose that stands alone as a symbol of perfection; the flowers are very full, flat and quartered, milky white with a touch of cream in the centre. 'Mrs Herbert Stevens', with her elegant fragrant white blooms, is another beauty in the Climbing Tea range, a daughter of the lovely white 'Frau Karl Druschki' and 'Niphetos'. 'Lady Hillingdon' is rather like a richly apricot-yellow form of 'Mrs Herbert Stevens', with the addition of dark foliage to set off the softly gracious blooms. The climbing form of 'Devoniensis' or the Magnolia Rose is another white Tea which can't be left out. In the words of Australian rosarian Judyth A. McLeod, 'this rose is pure clotted Devonshire cream!'

A couple of roses bred from *R. gigantea* earlier this century by Alister Clark of Melbourne, Australia, are still available from specialist nurseries: the large, single, cherry-tomato-red 'Nancy Hayward', and 'Lorraine Lee', a semi-double, warm apricot-pink. Both are vigorous plants with glossy green foliage and they flower well in warm climates.

BOURSAULTS AND BOURBONS

The Boursaults appeared in France early in the nineteenth century and are thought to have been the result of a union between *R. pendulina* and *R. chinensis*, the China Rose. Two of the Boursaults can still be found at old rose nurseries: 'Mme Sancy de Parabère, a vigorous thornless rose dating from 1874, with large flowers like a pink hollyhock; and 'Amadis', with smaller flowers of a deep rosy purple.

Then there are the Bourbons, also relatively thornless roses, making them useful for places where children play: 'Zéphirine Drouhin', a bright cerise-pink, and its soft pink sport 'Kathleen Harrop', which adorns the trellis by our sandpit. 'Blairii No. 2' is another pink Bourbon, deeper in the centre, and last but not least in the popularity stakes is the climbing form of

'Sombreuil'

'Souvenir de la Malmaison', with exquisite soft pink fully double quartered blooms, which excel if they can be sheltered from direct rain — under the eaves of a house, for example.

CLIMBING HYBRID TEAS

Some of these roses have occurred as climbing sports of Hybrid Teas, while others have been bred as climbers in their own right. Although some of them are not strictly speaking 'old' roses, there is a certain sense of nostalgia about them that qualifies them for inclusion. In some ways they are greatly improved when grown as climbers because they are softened by foreground planting instead of standing alone and bare in their own beds. Some of the romantic old reds come into this category, like 'Crimson Glory' and 'Étoile de Hollande', the incredibly dark, velvety 'Château de Clos Vougeot', 'Guinée' and 'Josephine Bruce'.

'Lady Waterlow' has soft, lightly veined blooms tinged with deeper coral-pink, while 'Mme Grégoire Staechelin' or 'Spanish Beauty' always gets strong praise for its appealing pink blooms with a deeper flush. Although a once-flowerer, it has many devotees because it puts on such a superb display, followed by wonderful golden orange hips in the autumn. 'Mme Caroline Testout' has a certain charm too, with its large cabbage-shaped silvery pink blooms. 'Shot Silk' is still a popular rose, coral-pink with yellow stamens, as

'Crimson Glory' (left) on fence around herb garden

44

'Étoile de Hollande'

is 'Paul's Lemon Pillar', offspring of 'Frau Karl Druschki' and 'Maréchal Niel', a mass of lavish lemony white scented blooms in spring.

And of course we can't forget that exquisite little miniature 'Cécile Brunner', the Sweetheart Rose, with its tiny perfectly scrolled pink buds paling to the softest pink as they open. The climbing form occurred as a sport from the bush form in 1894 in California. (It is more correctly a Hybrid China, as it is thought to be a cross between a Tea Rose and a Polyantha.)

MODERN CLIMBERS IN THE OLDER STYLE

Some roses in the latter part of this century have the sense of style and graciousness of the older varieties and are often found blending perfectly in gardens full of old roses. The emphasis here is on 'old-fashioned' rather than 'old'. To name but a few: 'Alchemist' (sometimes 'Alchymist') is almost a yellow form of 'Souvenir de la Malmaison', similar to 'Gloire de Dijon', while the almost-single 'Meg' is a stunning sight, with its large open apricot-peach blooms with pronounced stamens. 'Leverkusen' is a delightful pale yellow rose with interestingly uneven edges to its petals, and 'Maigold' is another Kordes rose with rich yellow blooms in abundance. The Austin rose 'Constance Spry' is always much admired, with its soft full clear pink flowers, well worth waiting for each year. 'Clair Matin' and 'Bantry Bay' are really useful pinks because they flower so freely, and 'Parade' is a deeper cerise with 'New Dawn' in its lineage. Another offspring of 'New Dawn', the perfectly

45

'Alchemist'   'Meg'

sculpted 'Pink Perpétue', can be very rewarding. It inherited its strong colouring from its other parent, the fiery red 'Danse de Feu'. 'Handel' is an interesting rose with its white flowers edged in a wine-pink shade; it is enhanced by other roses of that colour.

Ramblers

Broadly speaking, there are three main types of ramblers, named according to their ancestors: *R. sempervirens*, *R. multiflora* and *R. wichuraiana*. The oldest group, descendants of the Evergreen Rose, *R. sempervirens*, were raised around 1830. The Multiflora Ramblers appeared at the end of the nineteenth century, bringing us the purple 'Veilchenblau', 'Violette' and 'Bleu Magenta'. Many of the larger-flowered Wichuraiana Ramblers were bred in the early part of this century by Barbier in France, and the very different, smaller-flowered varieties by Jackson Perkins and M. H. Walsh in America.

SEMPERVIRENS RAMBLERS

Only two of the Sempervirens Ramblers are still readily available. 'Félicité et Perpétue', which bears masses of tiny white rosette-type flowers from pink buds, is a distinctive and vigorous old rose, very hardy despite its dainty appearance. It will be familiar to many people through the dwarf form, 'Little White Pet'. Its French breeder, M. Jacques, named it after his daughters, who were in turn named after the saints Felicitas and Perpetua. The other Sempervirens Rambler is 'Adélaide d'Orléans', an unforgettable rose whose double creamy pink flowers have often been described, accurately, as hanging in clusters just like the blossom on a Japanese cherry tree.

MULTIFLORA RAMBLERS

This group includes many old favourites. They are the kind of roses you wouldn't be without once you've grown them, and fortunately they can be grown in relatively small spaces if necessary; in fact, their trusses of small flowers suit a confined space. 'Veilchenblau', a bluish purple rose, looks superb grown against a creamy white wall or with other light-coloured roses. 'Tausendschön' or 'Thousand Beauties' is best described by Nancy Steen in her book *The Charm of Old Roses*: 'When the long branches are heavily laden with clusters of small flowers in several tones of pink, it is one of the loveliest sights in the garden, being greatly admired and much photographed.' The

'Adélaide d'Orléans'

47

now rather rare single pink 'Kathleen' is also an impressive sight. 'Tea Rambler', too, is a double soft pink fragrant rose which evokes a strong emotional response from those who grow it. One of my own favourites is 'Blush Rambler', which comes into flower later than most and has perfect soft pink flowers smothering each truss with a freshly simple appeal. 'Apple Blossom' is an aptly named pink rambler of similar innocence, as is the very old-fashioned looking, pale lilac-pink 'Lauré Davoust'. This is, in fact, one of the oldest of the Multifloras, dating from the early 1840s, and its flowers are a fascinating shape.

Two whites are 'White Flight' and 'Francis E. Lester', the latter opening from pink buds in early summer. The golden primrose-yellow 'Goldfinch' has a special charm, which it has passed on to its lovely seedling 'Ghislaine de Féligonde', a warm soft apricot-yellow.

WICHURAIANA RAMBLERS

The Wichuraiana Ramblers fall into two groups: those with larger flowers like 'Albertine', with glossy green foliage and fresh apple fragrance, and the smaller-flowered 'Dorothy Perkins' types, often seen on the side of the road in summer.

'Albertine' is so well known it scarcely needs description, a lovely rose with its coppery pink blooms so freely given on a very vigorous plant. Another pink of undeniable charm is 'François Juranville', an appealingly subtle rosy salmon, full flat and quartered; the depth of colour seems to vary depending on the conditions in which it is grown. 'Paul Transon' is more of a coppery

'Albertine'

'Paul Transon'

'Blush Rambler'

'Kathleen' (Multiflora, not Musk) growing through *Cotinus coggygria*, the smoke tree

salmon. Yet another rose bred by Barbier in France at the turn of the century is the superbly versatile and vigorous 'Albéric Barbier'. I have seen this rose as a giant hedge, covering old sheds, rambling down banks and hiding those very unattractive necessities, tennis-court fences. It has lovely lemon-yellow buds opening to white against a background of glossy green leaves. 'Emily Gray' supplies the yellow sample for this group, a soft buff shade of yellow ensuring its ongoing popularity.

The soft blush-pink 'New Dawn' made its appearance in 1930. Once established, it will cover a fence most effectively, tolerating some shade, although it doesn't always repeat as reliably as it's supposed to. 'Sea Foam' is a modern lax or trailing rambler with clusters of medium-sized double flowers, almost white blushed pink. It is extremely floriferous, making it a highly useful little rose.

'Dorothy Perkins', bred in the United States in 1902, is the best known of the smaller-flowered Wichuraianas, smothering itself in masses of tiny double bright pink flowers. There are several similar hybrids and a red version called 'Excelsa'. 'Sanders' White' is an exquisite white rambler with beautifully formed small double white flowers — lovely cascading from a standard or covering a pillar.

Wild Musk Roses

We can't leave the climbers and ramblers without mentioning a few of the wild roses still found in gardens today. *R. brunonii*, the Himalayan Musk or *R. moschata nepalensis*, for example, is an unforgettable sight late in spring, with

R. x *dupontii*

R. banksiae lutea, Yellow Banksia   *R. banksiae alba plena*, White Banksia

its clusters of single white flowers. *R.* x *dupontii* has long been a favourite of mine, lovely when growing into a tree, with its single white flowers and pronounced yellow stamens, soon darkening. Although a modern hybrid (1950), 'Wedding Day' fits in here, with its prolific clusters of single white flowers with orange-yellow stamens. Despite its rampant nature, it responds to the hedge clippers if necessary, seemingly without subsequent loss of flowers. Gertrude Jekyll and Vita Sackville-West used other rampant Musk Roses: 'The Garland', *R. longicuspis*, and *R. filipes* 'Kiftsgate', thereby preserving them for future generations.

Some species

BANKSIA ROSES

I am sure I share with thousands of other New Zealanders a childhood memory of a yellow Banksia flowering profusely every spring at the end of the verandah — a common sight but what an enchanting one! I now know that this was *R. banksiae lutea* from China, and I would hate to be without its abundance of tiny double yellow flowers borne in clusters on thornless branches, which keep most of their leaves. No doubt the verandah gave it some protection, but we had snow and frosts every winter so it must be relatively hardy.

The double white Banksia or *R. banksiae alba plena* is similar, and there are single forms: the yellow *R. banksiae lutescens* and the white *R. banksiae normalis*, which is supposed to be very fragrant. *R. fortuneana*, a larger-flowered white rose, was brought back from China by Robert Fortune around the middle of the last century and is thought to be a cross between the single Banksia and the Cherokee Rose, *R. laevigata*.

THE MACARTNEY ROSE

R. bracteata or the Macartney Rose is an extraordinary plant — more like a shrub than a rose, with its curiously blunted leaves and large bright white flowers centred round strong yellow stamens, which stand out beautifully against the healthy dense dark green foliage. However, it suckers madly and needs to be grown where it can't get out of hand; in parts of America it has become a problem. In the right spot it can clothe a wall most effectively, flowering continuously. Its offspring, the huge single yellow 'Mermaid', bred in 1918, has a growth habit in proportion to its amazing blooms once it gets established. These beautiful specimens, with their pronounced stamens, are produced continuously. In 1980 it gave rise to 'Pearl Drift', which is rapidly gaining popularity, and so it should as it is an excellent rose, low growing, dense and wide, bearing masses of white blooms with a tinge of pink inherited from its other parent, 'New Dawn'.

THE CHEROKEE ROSE

If you like single roses, the Cherokee Rose or *R. laevigata* is bound to captivate you. It has glossy green evergreen foliage and is one of the first roses to flower in spring, when it is a magnificent sight, with its large beautifully formed white flowers with yellow stamens. Once established in America, it became so at home that it gained the name Cherokee Rose and became the state flower of Georgia. There are pink and red hybrids, Anemone Rose or *R. anemonoides* and 'Ramona' or 'Red Cherokee' respectively, which are a little more generous with their flowers. *R. laevigata*'s most precious legacy, however, has been 'Silver Moon', with creamy white almost-single blooms emerging from yellow buds and produced in glorious abundance. What's more, they smell superbly of apples!

PART II

LANDSCAPING
WITH
OLD ROSES

CHAPTER 4

For small gardens

'…a purple patch or two…
to give an effect of colour.'
Horace

People with small gardens generally want patches of colour from spring to autumn, and with space at a premium old roses that flower over a long period, rather than for just a few weeks in spring, are in demand.

What better roses to start with than the Polyanthas? They grow well under a metre in height and flower repeatedly. The most popular of these is the rather overexposed 'The Fairy', which has large sprays of warm pink rosettes. 'Pinkie' is another pink but a much prettier looser flower, semi-double with a rich glowing tone, which produces large sprays of flowers all summer long on a very small compact plant. One of the best climbers for small gardens is the climbing sport of 'Pinkie', which reaches a height of up to 2.5 m, is always blooming and has the advantage of being almost thornless. Very soft powder-pink flowers cover 'Mignonette' on a plant that could be described as miniature. Constantly flowering, this rose makes an excellent small shrub. The larger-flowered Polyantha hybrid 'Mrs R. M. Finch' has in recent years become a very popular rose for the small garden. Growing to about 90 cm, it has medium-sized flowers of a warmish mid-pink, cupped and lightly double, and flowers continuously, thriving in quite dappled sunlight.

For white flowers, try 'Little White Pet', a sport of that incredibly invasive rambler 'Félicité et Perpétue'. With perfect little pure white rosettes opening from tiny red buds, it is a very prolific show-off and is useful because it does well in shade. Although it is not a Polyantha, its style and form allow it to fit in well with this group. 'Anna Maria de Montravel' is a smaller and much more informal double white flower, slightly taller and more upright in growth and therefore excellent for a restricted area.

'Mrs R. M. Finch'

'Complicata' (left), 'Strawberry Ice' (right) and unidentified rose on archway

'Cécile Brunner'

'Conchita' is a lightly double soft salmon-apricot Polyantha that deserves to be more widely grown. It was produced in 1935 by De Ruiter, who also produced 'Gloria Mundi', which has round flowers of rich orange. Another in this colour range is 'Pride of Hurst', which has rosettes of light salmon.

The Portland Roses 'Comte de Chambord', with its very double and highly perfumed deep rose-pink flowers, and 'Jacques Cartier', which is very similar in shape but has a lighter tone of pink, are both excellent for small gardens because of their compact growth and repeat flowering. Two others of this type that will do well are 'Arthur de Sansal', a very richly perfumed dark red, and 'Rose du Roi à Fleurs Pourpres', a red tinged with violet. All grow to 1 m.

The hybrid Chinensis are generally smallish compact roses and because of their long flowering period have become great garden favourites. One of the loveliest and most popular, 'Cécile Brunner', is a warm soft powder-pink that pales with age. Known as the Sweetheart Rose or the Buttonhole Rose, it has perfect little rosebuds used in wedding bouquets, head-dresses and buttonholes. A great favourite at Roseneath is the form with lemon-centred buds that open to pure white. Both these roses grow compact but upright to 1.5 m. A similar rose to these two is 'Perle d'Or', which is creamy apricot in colour and often described as the apricot or yellow form of 'Cécile Brunner'. When fully open, the petals unfurl, away from the centre, producing a raggy effect.

Although the climbing form of 'Cécile Brunner' is probably too vigorous for the small garden as it grows to about 8 m, a rose called 'Bloomfield Abundance' is an excellent small climber when carefully espaliered on a wall, growing to a height of 2 m. The main difference lies in the longer sepals, which supply just a touch of green around the flower when it is open. It also differs in growth habit, with shoots arising directly from the ground to form large fern-like sprays of flowers; these shoots must be cut out every couple of years so new ones will replace them. 'Marie Parvie' is one of the best of the early Polyanthas and one that grows well in shade. Always producing large clusters of little blooms of the palest pink, it has a slightly darker bud, fading to white before it drops. It is fragrant and practically thornless.

For a delicious perfume in a small garden, 'Comtesse du Cayla' is unsurpassed. A rose that could be likened to Joseph's coat, with its glowing colours of pink, apricot and orange touched with red, it does not have the harshness of colour of the pillar rose 'Joseph's Coat'. 'Comtesse du Cayla' grows to 1 m and tends to look a bit twiggy, but it is ideal for companion planting and has the added advantage of being constantly in flower. Another small climber in the Chinensis family is 'Fellemberg', which has rather muddled and loosely double flowers of a lavender-red. It is one of those roses that falls about, and this helps to make it a great little informal climber to a height of 2.5 m.

One of the roses I would not be without in a small garden is 'White Duchesse de Brabant', a sport of the warm shell-pink 'Duchesse de Brabant', also a good small-garden rose. The 'White Duchesse' opens with a pink glow through it and changes to pure white. As with many Teas it has a slightly

'Comtesse du Cayla'

weak neck and flowers that are cupped and loose. In frost-free climates both can flower for twelve months of the year.

'Hermosa' is a little rose with round buds that open to roundish flowers of lavender-pink, good for a shady spot, as is 'Mme Laurette Messimy', with its clusters of bright pink flowers that are ragged and lightly double.

'Semperflorens' is a good rich red, with smallish cupped flowers that are produced constantly on a small angular shrub. But if you want a dark velvet black-red, 'Louis XIV' is one of the deepest colours to be found. It is superb, although it needs a position with very lightly dappled shade as its petals tend to burn in strong sunlight. It is a beautiful rose but a bit temperamental, absolutely hating cold, wet and draughty sites.

Floribunda roses are excellent for companion planting, and with their heritage of the Polyantha behind them, they are almost constantly in flower. Although you could not call the hybrid 'Nancy Steen' an old rose, it certainly has that charm about it. A very fragrant rose of powder-pink with slightly warmer tones, growing to about 1 m, it is an excellent cutting rose. 'Gruss an Aachen' is one of the most beautiful roses that performs like a Floribunda, a small neat shrub with double flowers of the softest apricot-cream — a real winner, as is the pink form.

Many Floribundas produced through the 1950s and 1960s and up to the present day make good roses for small gardens, like the taller-growing 'Iceberg', which flowers prolifically with masses of loosely double medium-sized blooms, and the more beautiful 'Horstmann's Rosenresli'. The latter is a smaller and tidier plant with flowers that are more double than 'Iceberg', snow-white with a creamy tinge, opening gracefully with uneven-shaped petals.

'Gruss an Aachen'

'Pink Gruss an Aachen'

'Mme Laurette Messimy'

Although the rose 'Angel Face' was first released in 1968, it has a lot of attributes that make it fit well with old roses. Rich mauve with a lavender-lilac tone, the petals have a lightly frilled edge that is slightly darker in colour. The medium-sized flowers exude a spicy fragrance and are borne in clusters. At Omahanui, the Auckland garden of Toni and Ron Sylvester, I have seen this rose used to great advantage surrounded by blue perennials and the rose 'Yesterday', with its large clusters of small, almost-single flowers of lavender-purple. Another of the newer Floribundas with lavender-lilac toning and slightly more double than 'Angel Face' is 'Nightfall'. Although not quite as pretty as 'Angel Face', it has a purple tone in its thick green foliage, which makes it a very interesting plant to use in mixed borders.

Good yellow roses are hard to find for the small garden, but one that Sam McGredy produced in 1965 is standing the test of time well. 'Arthur Bell' has warm yellow loosely double flowers with a very rich perfume. Quite a small compact plant with plenty of foliage, which appears to be quite disease-resistant, it is a modern rose that has earned its place in many old-fashioned gardens.

While on the subject of modern roses, three more are recommended. 'Margaret Merril', which has beautiful pointed buds, is at its prettiest when half open. White blushed with pale pink, it looks like porcelain as it opens and has the added advantage of very spicy perfume. 'Ripples' is another lavender-mauve rose, softer in tone than 'Angel Face' and 'Nightfall', and with slightly larger flowers with loose petals. This is one of our visitors' favourite roses, as is the modern Tea 'Julia's Rose'. The colour of old brown lace, it has a bud that is rich copper in tone, and it is an excellent rose for flower arrangements.

Although I am not a great fan of the formality of standard roses, they can work well in the small garden if they are densely underplanted, as they provide height and shape. 'The Fairy' or any of the Polyanthas would be an excellent choice, as would 'Little White Pet', 'Marie Parvie', 'Gruss an Aachen' or 'Angel Face', but not 'Iceberg', as it gets too big for a small garden. The mini-weepers are ground-cover roses generally grafted onto a 1 m standard. These roses, like 'Snow Carpet' and 'Nozomi', are usually once-flowering so you must consider their use of space. Other procumbent roses such as 'Eyeopener' and 'Fairyland' are continuous-flowering but their use and placement in a small garden must also be carefully considered as they can be quite angular in growth.

The image of the modern Hybrid Tea Rose, with its sturdy upright growth and huge blooms that conjure up bright and almost gaudy colours, can be hard to accept, although some growers are now taking heed of the need for a softer style of flower. The older Tea hybrids include some great beauties, many very well suited to the sunny side of a small garden. A great favourite at

Archways provide extra planting opportunities and invite the visitor to explore partly hidden spaces in this densely planted small garden

'Fairyland'

Roseneath is the very dark red 'Francis Dubreuil', small and compact in growth with loose flowers and a rich tea perfume. 'Bon Silène' is slightly bigger in growth but still reasonably compact, and with its warm red flowers it makes an excellent choice in this colour range. If you are looking for roses with apricot tonings, the fragrant 'Gruss an Coburg' is a warm apricot colour not often found in old roses. Of quite strong and upright growth, like other Teas it prefers the sun.

Two white Teas are the compact bush 'Snowflake', with its pretty white flowers, and the even more beautiful but larger and more angular 'The Bride', which is a white sport of 'Catherine Mermet'. 'Catherine Mermet' would be my choice of two pink Teas; with the same growth pattern as 'The Bride', it has semi-double flowers of warm lavender-pink. Like its white sport, it is an excellent picking rose to have in a small garden. Another fine pink rose is the smaller-growing 'Maman Cochet', which is also a good cut flower. This rose is soft pink, loose and muddled — and not very thorny.

Three David Austin roses that do well and are now proven as good garden plants are 'Prospero', 'Wife of Bath' and 'Bredon'. 'Prospero' is a small compact plant, with the flowers held directly upright in clusters. They emerge from their buds of deep rich red, exuding a strong rose perfume, to form flat flowers that are slightly reflexed; they hold their shape and slowly

61

A successful grouping of roses and companion plants in a
confined area within an urban garden

change colour to a deep warm violet-burgundy-red. This rose flowers constantly in a warm climate, although it is said not to perform well in colder
areas. The delightful 'Wife of Bath', with its warm pink cupped flowers, has
also proved itself in our garden, as has 'Bredon', with its soft apricot-buff-
yellow flowers of similar form to 'Prospero'. These three roses belie the words
of those who say that English roses all have flowers that are far too big.

Finally, here are some suggestions for roses that can be used as climbers
or against walls. The almost thornless 'Adam' is a very old English Tea, one of
the first, which does particularly well as a climber in a warm and protected
small garden. Quite big and blowzy, of soft salmon and apricot shades, it has
survived 160 years, which says a lot as many modern hybrids last only a few
seasons before they are dropped from sales lists.

'Mme Jules Gravereaux' is another beauty, this time from Luxembourg,
which is displayed well against a sunny wall of stained wood. The flowers are
quite large, buff with a golden tone and tinged with apricot. 'Souvenir d'un
Ami' is a very large shrub rose that grows well against a wall, reaching a
height of 3 m. Often bought as a gift for someone who has lost a loved one, it
is a truly magnificent rose, with very tightly packed double flowers of old
dark rose-pink with an apricot tinge and a satin sheen as well as a rich
perfume.

'Pax', a big loosely double white Hybrid Musk that grows to 2.5 m,
makes an excellent climber. With its Musk parentage, it tolerates a shady
wall very well and flowers continuously. Also loosely double is 'Dawning', a
soft mid-pink with a yellow flush at the base of the petals. Growing to 3.5 m,

it is almost thornless. A yellow climber that needs the warmth of a sunny wall and the love of a patient gardener to perform well is 'Solfaterre'. A temperamental Noisette with big soft sulphur flowers, it is a refined rose, well worth the care it needs.

Classed as a modern rose, the great American beauty 'Aloha' (1949) has the graceful soft silver-pink 'New Dawn' as a parent, and it certainly lives up to its parentage. Constantly in flower, this stunning rose has large many-petalled blooms that are very richly perfumed. A warm rose-pink with apricot and darker rose tonings, it is superb for a small garden's arch or pergola, and wonderful in a silver rose bowl in the middle of a dinner table.

The circular design of this tiny space means that the garden may be viewed from several different angles as well as providing access to the densely planted perimeter

CHAPTER 5

For large gardens

'It was roses, roses, all the way.'
Robert Browning

The majority of old roses grow into large shrubs, and many grow into wild and unruly plants. The beauty of having a large garden is being able to allow them the space to grow as they do in their natural state. Many have a short flowering season and people with small gardens are often loath to give them space because of this. In a large garden, planting schemes can more easily take this into consideration, and by carefully planting these brief-flowering roses with those that will flower through the seasons of spring, summer and autumn into winter, you can have the effect of roses, roses all the way.

Many brief-flowering climbers deserve a place in the large garden. One of the most graceful of these is the soft silver-pink, single climbing Hybrid Tea 'Cupid'. Draped along a trellis, it scatters its flowers intermittently along its branches — it is as if the plant realises that it needs to set its beautiful blooms off against its dark foliage. Planted on the same trellis as the Wichuraiana hybrid 'Dr W. van Fleet', 'Cupid' will have finished its spring flowering before its companion produces its loosely double, pale satin-pink flowers early in the summer. 'Dr W. van Fleet' sported the ever-popular 'New Dawn', which flowers and grows in exactly the same way but will repeat through until autumn.

Another single and brief-flowering Wichuraiana hybrid is the palest of pale creamy butter-yellow 'Jersey Beauty'. This rose is ideal for a trellis, pergola or tall pillar in a big garden, for it will trail 5–6 m quite easily. For a contrast of colour in the spring, 'Jersey Beauty' planted with the dramatic, once-flowering 'Mme Alice Garnier', with its double flowers of bright salmon-pink, will provide a wonderful display. A 'Jersey Beauty' seedling, 'Emily Gray' is also only once-flowering but well worth giving space to. It has very picturesque fragrant yellow flowers that are semi-double. This rose is best planted by itself, as it is a very strong grower with dense glossy green foliage that contrasts well against the yellow flowers. This is a rose that will literally smother a trellis for 6 m.

Two good dark red roses that flower in spring are the very double-flowered and aptly named 'Crimson Glory' and 'Guinée'. The latter is a much darker red velvet flower that is not as heavy-petalled as 'Crimson Glory'. Both these roses exude a heady perfume and are ideal for potpourri. If you are lucky, 'Guinée' will provide a second flowering in autumn. Vigorous in growth, they will both climb to 5–6 m. 'Crimson Glory' is a parent of 'Cerise Bouquet', a massive shrub rose that grows to a clump at least 3 m high and 3 m wide. With fragrant double red flowers covering the shrub in spring, it becomes a wonderful specimen but it definitely needs a large garden to be seen to advantage.

There are lots of species and their early hybrids that, at their best, are wild and unruly. *R. roxburghii* is one of these. It is not a popular garden plant, as it is quite shy when it comes to producing its very double rose-pink flowers. In spite of this, it is a very interesting bush, with its stiff angular growth pattern and fern-like foliage, and it is one of the few roses to have peeling bark. Given space, it will grow to 2 m or more, but because of its thorns it needs to be in a position where it can be given a wide berth when you are weeding or mowing. In contrast to the thorns of *R. roxburghii*, the

'Ballerina'

'Miss Muffet' growing out of a hedge, with 'Maxima',
climbers 'Pink Perpétue' and 'Uetersen', 'Marie de Blois' and
'William Lobb' in foreground, and 'Common Moss' on left

North American species *R. nutkana* is almost thornless, and its charming flowers are single, of a warm lavender-pink. Allowed to grow to its full size in a garden, it will become a shrub of 2.5 m.

Many species are budded onto a *multiflora* stock, not only because the stock has a good root system but because this stops them from suckering. If you have the space, the normal growth habits of roses growing on their own roots create plants that have a much more natural shape and balance. This is well seen in the single-flowered and hip-producing *R. moyesii* and *R. sweginzowii*. Budded onto stock, they will send out four or five 3 m long branches, resulting in a tall, lanky and bare-looking shrub waving in the breeze. If allowed the space to grow on their own rootstock, they will form very large dense shrubs at least 2.5 m wide. Plants of these two species, several years old, have no equal when smothered in hundreds of their vase-shaped hips. Another species with the same growth pattern is the very pretty single yellow-flowered *R. hugonis*. With a multitude of thorns, it looks brilliant in autumn as its ferny foliage changes colour and it displays its rich red hips.

Another rose with good autumn foliage, *R. rugosa* looks its best when allowed to form a dense clump on its own roots. It has tall straight canes over 2 m high and becomes quite impenetrable. Beware, though, if you have light or sandy soil, for it will take over the garden if allowed. There are numerous forms of this rose. Often found growing in sand dunes, *R. rugosa* and its many types and hybrids are tolerant of sea spray.

Many old roses are excellent plants to use in shrubberies, where their flowers offset the foliage of other plants, and there are none better for this than the Bourbons. 'Souvenir de Mme Brieul', with its large double rich rose-pink flowers, is one of the best, its long (2.5 m) branches becoming weighed down with its heavy and very fragrant flowers. 'Adam Messerich', which has loosely double red flowers, grows to about 2 m on a more erect plant and, like most Bourbons, will flower continuously through the seasons. Those who are interested in striped roses will not be able to go past 'Commandant Beau-repaire', which has rich red flowers that are striped with white and pink. The other striped Bourbon is 'Honorine de Brabant', an exquisite rose which has large double flowers of the palest lavender-pink with purple stripes. It will sprawl to 2.5 m and is ideal to drape along a fence.

Although the Moss Roses do not do particularly well in warm climates, I would never be without 'William Lobb' trained somewhere along a fence. It is one of the most radiant and richly coloured of all roses. Often called 'Old Velvet', it certainly deserves this title, with its flowers that have tones of purple, lilac and red. The flowers simply glow, and drops of rain on them look like precious stones; semi-double, they are borne on vigorous branches. It is at its best espaliered on a fence, which enables a multitude of flowers to be produced along the branches rather than just at the tops, as would be the case if it were allowed to grow in an erect fashion.

The rose is the jewel of the garden, and the Gallicas are some of the most

'Poulsen's Park Rose' on the right is balanced by the purple form of annual *Salvia horminum* in the bed on the left and *R. multiflora simplex* in the background

splendid, even though they have a very brief flowering period — here one month, gone the next. For those who are interested in very old hybrid roses, the ancient *R. gallica violacea* ('La Belle Sultane'), with its almost-single flowers of soft burgundy offset by soft golden stamens, is one of the most beautiful. This shrub is definitely best in a mixed border or shrubbery, for when it is not flowering in mid-spring it is a rather bare-looking plant. 'Oeillet Parfait' is also an untidy-looking plant, with flowers of white with red stripes that are very double. Also worth growing in a shrubbery, where its shyness will not be too noticeable, is the stunning 'Belle de Crécy'. If it decides to display its lovely fragrant double flowers of pink and lavender, it is one of the delights of the garden. Another appealing Gallica is the 'Empress Josephine', which has double rose-pink flowers that have soft lilac and pink tonings. This rose bush tends to flop about all over the place, and although it needs space, it is best placed among other shrubs where it will gain support. A rose that may be a Gallica, but is possibly an *R. macrantha* hybrid, is the popular and very beautiful single pink 'Complicata'. It can be used on a pillar or a fence, or as a sprawling shrub. A bonus is its autumn display of hips.

David Austin has produced the *R. macrantha* hybrid 'Chianti', a once-flowering purple-red double rose that is very fragrant and deserves to be more popular than it is. Growing to 1.5 m, it is a welcome addition to any border.

The Centifolias are some of the loveliest roses there are. As a specimen,

'Joseph's Coat' on left, 'Lamarque' behind, 'Graham Thomas' and 'Yellow Charles Austin' at the back and 'Windrush' in the front

'Chianti'   'Nevada'

'Fantin-Latour', set in the centre of a large bed or just growing on its own, is certainly one of the most handsome and a must in a large garden. On its own roots it will grow into a huge shrub 1 m across at its base, sending up tall shoots of 2–2.5 m which, in late spring, are massed with double flowers of warm glowing pink. Typical of the Centifolias, the blooms are quartered and large, and they issue forth the most generous of perfume. Also strongly fragrant is the famous Centifolia 'Tour de Malakoff', a superb rose of rich light burgundy which acquires a dark lavender tone as it ages. Good as a cut flower, it is often found in old still-life paintings of fruit and flowers.

The Albas add great charm to any garden, with their sweetly scented, softly coloured flowers on large shrubs that often have slightly glaucous foliage. If you are partial to single roses because of their simplicity, then the White Rose of York is one of the best. The shrub is over 2 m in height, very erect in growth, and when scattered with its single white flowers it has a certain refinement to it. *R.* x *alba* 'Maxima' is a very charming double white flower, probably much older than the single White Rose of York. A lot of the Albas are tolerant of shade, including 'Félicité Parmentier', 'Chloris' and 'Celestial'. 'Félicité Parmentier' is the smallest growing of the three (to 1.5 m) and is also suitable for small gardens; it has very double flowers of softest pale pink. 'Chloris' has flowers which are not quite so full of petals and are a slightly richer glowing pink; it is also slightly taller. Even taller growing again is the ever-popular 'Celestial', often known as 'Céleste', which has lightly double flowers of a paler rosier pink and is very rich in perfume. 'Mme Plantier', which is known as the Bridal Rose because of its beautiful button-eyed off-white flowers, is also called the Cemetery Rose in New Zealand as it is often found in old cemeteries. Keep this rose in check with a pair of hedge-clippers. I have *Agapanthus* 'Storm Cloud' growing through 'Mme Plantier'; the agapanthus flowers later than the rose, and the dark blue flowers of 'Storm Cloud' sit well against the Alba's foliage.

Damask Roses are flowers of great splendour. They are good for growing in shrubberies, where most, if planted in smallish spots, will grow upright and hold their flowers out above the foliage. Who would be without 'Mme Hardy' or 'Ispahan'? One of the most beautiful white roses ever produced is 'Mme Hardy', resplendent with medium-sized very double flowers with a green button eye. It will clothe a trellis to a height of 2.5 m in warmer climates, but as a bush it should be kept pruned to 1.8 m or so. 'Ispahan' conjures up visions of Vita Sackville-West and Harold Nicholson trekking through Persia. A rose from that area, it grows into a bush over 2 m high and upright, the tall shoots being weighed down with warm pink blooms in late spring. With spring rains and warm spring sun, you can catch its heady perfume as you walk near it. 'Leda' or the Painted Damask is an unusual flower, of the palest pink, almost white, with a button eye. The outer edges of the petals have dark red tinges, hence the name Painted Damask. A very low-growing shrub, it will easily cover a square metre of ground and is excellent on the end of a long bed. 'Botzaris' is a luscious, very double, muddled white flower that is a must in a big garden.

Hybrid Perpetuals were produced over a period of fifty years, from approximately 1840 to 1890. It is slightly misleading to call them perpetual, a term more fitted to the Chinas; at most I would say they are recurrent. 'Baroness Rothschild', with its large satin-pink flowers, is one of the classics, and like its progeny 'Gloire Lyonnaise', a lightly double white with a softest cream hue, prefers to be only lightly underplanted. 'Mrs John Laing' produces lovely buds that form flowers of quite uniform shape, a warm rich pink. These three roses all grow to 1.5 m and make quite good specimens in a lightly mixed border. 'Ferdinand Pichard' is slightly more lax in growth and produces smaller flowers than those previously mentioned but in much greater quantity. It is quite a good rose to use on a low fence. If you like striped roses, this is the most striking, with its very sharply contrasting colours of strong red, soft pink and flecks of white; the blooms are musk-scented.

'Aimée Vibert' is one of the loveliest of all the Noisettes, and in late summer it will trail off the top of a 3 m high pergola with long whip-like branches. The flowers are medium-sized and are offset by contrasting small round red buds, which open to pure white very double blooms. 'Desprez à Fleurs Jaunes' is a soft warm apricot rose which is double and loosely quartered. Vigorous in growth, reaching 8 m along the top of a trellis, it is a good rose to grow on a two-storey house.

One of the luxuries of a big garden is being able to plant two or three

'Jean Ducher'

'Félicité et Perpétue'

roses of the same variety together to form a large clump or the impression of a huge shrub, as we have done with 'Général Galliéni'. These old Tea Roses perform well from mid-summer onwards when the weather is drier. On a large shrub of 1.5 m the roses vary in colour depending on the climate; they can be totally red or buff, or a mix of the two with tones of pink. The flowers are well offset by the dull olive foliage. 'Jean Ducher' is one of the most popular of all Tea Roses and does well in a grouping of three. Flowering continuously on a large shrub of 2 m, it has blooms which are large, blowzy and loosely double, of an exceptionally pale apricot with pale pink tonings. A good rule with these large-flowered roses, if you have the space, is to let the bush grow large in proportion to the flowers; nothing looks worse than large blooms on a small and heavily pruned bush.

CHAPTER 6

For pillars, arches and pergolas

'Blossom by blossom the spring begins.'
Algernon Charles Swinburne

Spring is the season of romance, and what more romantic place is there than a garden of roses? Trellis, arches, pillars, pergolas and summerhouses help shape a garden, adding structure and providing height for climbing roses. Plants smothered in blossom, trailing, cascading and foaming over these structures, make the spring garden a very romantic place.

A pillar rose is either a small climber or a large shrub rose, such as 'Sparrieshoop', both pink and white forms, and the sharply coloured 'Joseph's Coat'. These roses will quite easily stand alone and do not need support, but concentrated on a pillar or arch, they can make a dramatic focal point. 'Sparrieshoop' is an excellent rose, repeatedly flowering all through spring, summer and early autumn with heads of medium-sized single rose-pink flowers. The white form has cream flowers tinged with pink as they age. 'Joseph's Coat' is a relatively modern rose in orange and yellow, colours not often found in old roses. Semi-double and repeating well, it is a very popular bright flower that adds excitement and interest to a garden.

Many gardeners prefer more lax-growing roses like *R. macrantha*, 'Raubritter' and *R.* x *dupontii* as pillar roses because they tend to hang loosely off the pillar, giving a much more relaxed look than the upright and angular-growing varieties. A favourite with many people is the Noisette 'Céline Forestier', which has reasonably large flowers, very double, soft lemon-yellow and exuding a delectable perfume. Growing to a height of 3 m and repeating constantly, it has soft light lime-green foliage which offsets the flowers perfectly. 'Blush Noisette' also makes an excellent pillar rose; it is loosely

73

'White Sparrieshoop'

Roses and wisteria growing on archways

double and warmish blush-pink. The Noisettes really perform well in sunny spots but certain ones are quite tolerant of shade, 'Mme Alfred Carrière' being the most popular of these. This sweetly scented rose will grow to 6 m and is excellent for walls or very tall pillars as it tends to keep sending its growing shoots upwards. It looks spectacular smothered in blossom on a 2.5 m trellis but needs constant attention to keep it in check. A medium-sized loosely double white rose with a pale pink blush, it flowers prolifically all through the seasons and in warmer climates into winter.

'Lamarque' is an exceptional climbing Noisette, in its element in hot climates. In a sunny situation it produces a multitude of powerfully perfumed large very double roses, which open up with an almost greenish tinge and turn to pure snow-white offset by dull lime-green foliage.

'Maréchal Niel' is a warm yellow Noisette that is one of our great favourites, but it must be grown under the cover of a verandah or something similar to do well.

'Crépuscule' flowers continuously through three seasons, with smallish double flowers of loosely held petals in orange-apricot. 'Cloth of Gold', which has large blowzy double blooms of butter-gold and comes with the recommendation of being a seedling from 'Lamarque', is an aromatically perfumed rose for a trellis in direct sun as it is definitely a sun-loving variety. Worth pampering, it does particularly well in warmer climates.

A fault of many climbing Hybrid Teas and other modern climbers is that they hold their flowers stiffly upwards, so often only the underside of the rose is visible. One of the worst is the most beautiful single strawberry-pink 'Dainty Bess'. With its lightly frilled petals and deep brownish strawberry anthers, it is a real stunner: if it were not for its definite upright growth in both the bush and climbing forms, it would get 10 out of 10. It is at its best where it can be seen from above, on a pergola at the bottom of a long sloping walk, or trained along below eye level. A climbing white Hybrid Tea that is an excellent choice is 'Mrs Herbert Stevens'. Being weak in the stem, it hangs its head and you can easily look up into the flowers. The slightly largish pointed buds look wonderful as they start to unfurl, opening to reasonably large loose flowers with that lovely tea scent.

'Mme Caroline Testout' is another climbing Hybrid Tea that has stood the test of time, being a 1901 sport from the 1890 bush form from Pernet-Ducher. Satin-pink and very well scented, it is one of those large globular roses often erroneously called Cabbage Roses. 'Ulrich Brunner Fils' also fits this description. It is a deep dull red in colour, growing to 2 m, and can be used as a small climber. Pernet-Ducher have given us the best of these early climbing Teas, another being the 1913 'Mme Édouard Herriot' or the 'Daily Mail Rose' (although the climbing form was released by Ketter Bros of Luxembourg in 1921). An unusual rosy salmon colour, it is lightly double and tea scented with an irresistible charm.

'Souvenir de Mme Léonie Viennot', recently reintroduced to England from New Zealand, is warm pink with a soft yellow base to the petals. Vigorous in growth to 6 m, it is a mass of flowers in spring, repeating well all through summer to autumn — a good rose for warm climates. 'Château de Clos Vougeot' is a rose of great beauty with a balmy perfume, but it looks untidy and is best on a trellis behind, say, a cottage garden planting, where this ugly duckling of a plant can be softened and the beauty of its dark red velvet blooms fully revealed.

A rose that is irresistible to many people is the climbing form of 'Souvenir de la Malmaison'. This Bourbon, also known as 'The Queen of Beauty and Fragrance', is the palest of pinks and has a lovely bud that slowly unfurls. It is at its best half open, with loose petals on the outside and the unfolding bud still in the centre; at this stage it has a slightly deeper colour. When it is fully blown, with its multitude of petals, it is very blowzy. At the thought of rain 'Souvenir de la Malmaison' balls, turns brown and rots, and in humid climates it is susceptible to powdery mildew. But in spite of all this, it can have perfect blooms, even in mid-winter.

Two other Bourbons that are great climbers are also thornless — 'Zéphirine Drouhin' and 'Kathleen Harrop'. 'Zéphirine Drouhin' is lightly double and a warm reddish pink, exuding that ambrosial Bourbon fragrance. Growing to a height of 4 m, it is best for a pergola that needs a continuous splash of colour as a focal point. 'Kathleen Harrop' is a much softer pink sport of 'Zéphirine Drouhin' with exactly the same growth pattern. These Bourbons definitely like air movement around them as they are all susceptible to mildew.

One of the first roses in our collection, which was started 25 years ago,

'New Dawn'

'Sanders' White' grown as a standard (in autumn)

'Applejack' with *Cheiranthus* 'Joy Gold' and lime-green
Euphorbia coralloides on left, with 'Paul Transon' in the background

77

Red 'Général Galliéni' and yellow 'Céline Forestier'

was the Wichuraiana hybrid 'New Dawn'. Many people, and we tend to agree with them, say there has never been a better-flowering pink rose. The plant is smothered in warm powder-pink lightly double blooms from late spring, and with attention to dead-heading — it sets hips very quickly — it will flower continuously until autumn. Although spectacular over an archway in full sun, it also flowers well in shade. 'Parade' is a seedling from 'New Dawn' which produces lightly perfumed flowers with many more petals than its famous parent; they are quite a strong rich cerise-pink colour — not everyone's favourite. Great as either a pillar or a climber, like its parent it is good in shade.

In old roses apricot and salmon colours are hard to find, so 'Aviateur Blériot' is a breath of fresh air if you are looking for these tonings. It produces great sprays of dainty, sweetly scented apricot-cream flowers, which fade to cream with age. 'Copper Glow' is a deep apricot-orange, with well-shaped pointed buds opening to a lightly double flower. These flowers have long stems and when in bud are good as a cut flower. 'Alchemist', a large fully double flower of peachy apricot-yellow, well deserves a place in any garden, even though it is only once-flowering. Constantly in flower through the seasons is 'William Allen Richardson'. With its clusters of apricot blooms, this rose grows to about 3 m and needs a sheltered spot to really flourish.

Another very pretty Wichuraiana hybrid is 'Crimson Showers'. With small round flowers of rich crimson hanging in large clusters from the whip-like branches, it looks good trained to the top of a 4 m high trellis and allowed to fall freely. 'Dorothy Perkins', the pink roadside rambler, and 'Excelsa', its red counterpart, are similar in habit but need a slightly lower trellis; care is needed with these two roses as they tend to take over and become weeds.

Good red climbers like 'Crimson Glory', 'Josephine Bruce', and 'Étoile de Hollande' are mentioned in the chapter on perfumes; there are others, 'Monsieur Tillier' being one of the best. This rose was bred in France by Bernaix in 1891 and is a glowing crimson with occasional white and violet flecking. It has a mild but delicious tea scent and flowers constantly from very early spring. In warm climates it grows well on a trellis, up to 2.5 m in each direction, but in cooler climates it tends to remain as a small shrub. The true 'Monsieur Tillier' was only recently introduced to New Zealand by Peter Beales through Tasman Bay Roses; until then the bush rose 'Archiduc Joseph', which was produced in France by Nabonnand in 1872, had been wrongly sold in New Zealand as 'Monsieur Tillier'. 'Archiduc Joseph' is another beautiful Tea, large and many-petalled, and an unusual and subtle blend of apricot-pink-salmon with an equally unusual scent; this does not come as a climber. In hot dry climates it flowers extremely well and continuously. 'Reine Marie Henriette' is an excellent climber, with pointed buds and large lightly double flowers of rich warm violet-red which are sweetly scented. It flowers abundantly and continuously, and will grow to about 4 or 5 m.

Some of David Austin's English Roses are best grown as climbers. The most magnificent of these is 'Graham Thomas', a rose truly worthy of the

'White Sparrieshoop' and 'Mrs Herbert Stevens' on a
summerhouse

79

'Emily Gray' on a pillar

OTHER ROSES FOR PILLARS,
ARCHES & PERGOLAS

'Achievement'	'Gardenia'
'Adam'	'Ghislaine de
'Aimée Vibert'	Féligonde'
'Albéric Barbier'	'Gloire de Dijon'
'American Pillar'	'Guinée'
'Bantry Bay'	'Jersey Beauty'
'Black Boy'	'Lady Waterlow'
'Champneys' Pink	'Mme P. S. Dupont'
Cluster'	'Mme Grégoire
'Charles Austin'	Staechelin'
'Clair Matin'	'May Queen'
'Constance Spry'	'Moonlight'
'Dortmund'	'Niphetos' (climbing)
'Elmshorn'	'Paul's Lemon Pillar'

honour of its name. Growing up to 4.5 m and repeating well, it smothers itself with large, many-petalled but loosely shaped flowers of deep rich golden yellow that exude a strange and unusual perfume. With blue clematis growing through it, the contrast is electrifying. 'Abraham Darby' is not quite so vigorous but grows to 2.5 m. Also many-petalled and loosely flowered, it is salmon-apricot and has a strong rose perfume. 'Leander' is another David Austin rose that does well as a small climber. A darker apricot than 'Abraham Darby', it has a more old-fashioned, almost quartered style, and is also highly rose-scented.

One excellent and very old rose is 'Old Blush China'. Always in flower unless hit by a winter frost, it has smallish floppy double flowers of satin-rose-pink. The climbing form is not as well known as the bush variety; it reaches 4.5 m and does well as a bushy climber in a shrubbery. 'Indica Major', a once-flowering hybrid of this species, is a most attractive rose, with double flowers that are creamy white and tinged with pink but, sadly, not scented. Also excellent for scrambling through a shrubbery, it is always in flower early in the season before most spring roses. Staying with the Chinensis roses, the small-flowered lilac-pink 'Pompon de Paris' is an excellent little climber, quite upright in growth; it can also be trained to grow as a hedge.

People are often heard to say, 'I'd love that rose but I don't have any more room for climbers'. There is a solution: put in a 2–3 m post and plant a climbing rose beside it. As the rose grows, twine it around the post and then let it fall freely from the top. It looks very informal and gives your garden a more romantic feeling.

CHAPTER 7

For growing into trees, over fences and buildings

'Flung roses, roses, riotously . . .'
Ernest Dowson

Roses covering an unsightly shed or tumble-down fence can make quite a statement in the garden when they cover these features with a blanket of leaves and flowers. Mix the colours, and with sharp contrasts the roses will create a riot of colour and draw the eye from the object that is being disguised.

Roses in trees, both deciduous and evergreen, add a new dimension to a garden, giving splashes of colour against the green foliage. If possible, it's preferable to plant the rose at the same time as the tree.

One of the most popular varieties for growing into trees is 'Wedding Day', with its large sprays of single white flowers followed by great clusters of small round orange fruit. It easily reaches a height of 12 m and is very showy when displaying its foaming blossoms along great trailing stems.

'Albertine' is one of the best loved of all ramblers, even though it flowers for a very short period. Its masses of loose double flowers of a rich rose-pink with soft salmon-apricot tonings release a luscious perfume into the garden. 'Félicité et Perpétue' was planted with an ornamental pear fourteen years ago at Roseneath and now the tree and the rose are over 6 m high. Masses and masses of small off-white rosettes emerge from small round red buds, cascading downwards on long trailing branches. With dark reddish green foliage, this is one of the most vigorous and dense of roses, and one that is perfect for smothering an unsightly garden shed.

A charming little rose that ambles through trees is 'Lauré Davoust', with its small lavender-pink pompom-like flowers. A graceful climber such as this, wandering through a tree, hedge or shrubbery, is much more visually pleasing

81

than a trifid-like rambler that takes over. A hybrid of *R. foetida*, 'Lawrence Johnston' produces medium-sized and buttercup-yellow flowers and is set off well against rich green leaves. It is richly fragrant, unlike its 'foetid' parent. 'Le Rêve' has the same parentage as 'Lawrence Johnston' but is best grown as a large shrub in a shrubbery.

Most Teas are not suitable for planting in trees, but 'Souvenir de Mme Léonie Viennot' is one that does well. Planted beside an almond at Roseneath, it hangs out of the tree in many places, including the shaded side, and flowers on the ends of its branches, which makes it well suited for trailing through shrubberies.

Some gardeners prefer roses that drape themselves lightly through trees — like *R. gentiliana*, with its lightly pink-blushed white single flowers, or *R. chinensis*, a single red-rose-pink. *R. laevigata rosea*, with its glossy green foliage and large waxy rose-pink single flowers, is excellent in trees but needs to be planted on a sunny sheltered side to do really well. *R. laevigata*, with its single white flowers and the same growth habit, is slightly more vigorous.

The lavender-violet-purple tones of the roses 'Violette', 'Veilchenblau' and 'Bleu Magenta', which grow to a height of 6 m, are well suited to the colour of light green-leaved trees. Two other very beautiful Multiflora Ramblers are 'Francis E. Lester' and 'Bobbie James'. 'Francis E. Lester' has large sprays of single white flowers which open with strong pink tones on the petal edges; these fade as the flowers age, creating a soft hazy pink effect in a small tree. 'Bobbie James' is a relatively new hybrid that deserves to become much more widely planted. Semi-double and white with a very pale cream toning, the flowers fall lightly from the tree in large clusters. Put a seat under this tree and catch the perfume in the air.

The Banksias are some of the best roses to use in a tree or over a large building. They do well in warm climates, but in areas which get snow and frost they need a bit of pampering on warm walls. They take a few years to get to a reasonable height before they start to flower well but they are worth the effort. *R. banksiae lutea*, which has no perfume, will grow up to 10 m, with small double buttery yellow flowers in large clusters. With long trailing shoots, it hangs wonderfully from trees, as does the single yellow form, *R. banksiae lutescens*, which is lightly scented. The white single *R. banksiae normalis* is just as vigorous as these other forms, and a great advantage is that they are all completely thornless. 'Banksia Purezza', a more recent (1961) hybrid, has much larger double blooms than the earlier forms and they have a rich fragrance, as does the 'Banksia Hybride di Castello', a cross between *lutescens* and that beautiful Noisette 'Lamarque'. With the latter as a parent, 'Banksia Hybride di Castello' repeats its flowering well. Another beautifully perfumed rambler is the violet-scented *R. banksiae alba plena*. With its clusters of creamy white flowers and very sprawling growth habit, it is ideal for smothering an unsightly fence.

R. bracteata and 'Mermaid' are the best of the evergreen roses for

'Wedding Day' with 'François Juranville'

'Lauré Davoust'

83

R. laevigata

enveloping structures. *R. bracteata*, covering a wall and neatly clipped around the opening of doors and windows, is the most successful of all roses for this treatment. 'Mermaid' is more reckless in its growth habit, better suited to an old barn or garage. Watch the thorns on these; there are very few other roses that are quite as vicious.

The rambler 'Shower of Gold', not to be confused with 'Golden Showers', is another good dense grower for concealing a fence or shed. It will reach a height of 7 m then cascade down with long shoots covered in flowers of soft gold fading to pale yellow. With its dark green foliage, it makes a good feature. Another good yellow for trees, and remember that yellow and green harmonise well, is 'Easlea's Golden Rambler'. Loosely double and butter-cup-yellow, it is most striking in trees as it grows to a height of 6 m. Although tolerant of shade, these roses all tend to head for the sun, given half a chance.

A beautiful rose that will cover the face of a building is the vigorous 'Silver Moon'. It has rich green foliage, and when it is in full bloom, with large single white flowers, it is like a great white waterfall — a very exuberant rose indeed. Another white rose that is great for hiding something is 'Sanders' White'. In New Zealand a lot of old homes used to have outside lavatories; in fact some survive in country areas and certain older city suburbs. These small buildings were often at the end of a long path directly opposite the back door and shrubs were planted to disguise them. The most successfully disguised that I have seen was smothered in 'Sanders' White'. The lavatory had a pole on top, which the rose had been allowed to climb and then trail down. Parted over the doorway like a pair of curtains, it looked more like a summerhouse than an outside lavatory when covered in its ample foliage and small white rosettes.

Unsightly concrete walls can be effectively disguised with *R. glauca*, which has glaucous foliage richly toned with purple and wine. This rose is a real delight, with its warm-coloured leaves and small, pretty dull rose-pink flowers followed by hanging clusters of wine-tinged-red hips. *R. arvensis*, with its single white flowers with gold stamens and tracery of branches, also looks great against grey concrete, as does 'Dortmund', which has lush shiny green leaves and large rich red single flowers. 'Dortmund' has the advantage of being recurrent, and it is a much smaller-growing rose than the two previously mentioned.

Two varieties good for untidy looking fences are 'Leverkusen' and 'Parkdirektor Riggers'. 'Leverkusen' is a very dense plant with shiny green foliage that offsets the soft yellow flowers well. 'Parkdirektor Riggers' is not quite as dense, with semi-double flowers which are quite a sharp glowing red that is hard to place with other colours. The flowers are offset against a rich reddish green foliage. Used against a fence or shed, it becomes quite a striking feature.

I recently saw an example of an inspired planting, where two more modern roses, 'Michèle Meilland' and 'Sutter's Gold', were intermingled on a very large barn. What a sight! Growing two storeys high and many metres across, the soft apricot-pink of 'Michèle Meilland' and the yellow-flamed-with-orange 'Sutter's Gold' made a delightful combination against the dull red-painted barn.

'Albéric Barbier'

'Desprez à Fleurs Jaunes'

The Wichuraiana hybrid 'Mary Wallace' is another good rose to use if you want to cover an old shed. Loosely double, sweetly scented, lavender-pink and just covered in bloom, it will thickly cover anything, as will 'François Juranville', which is a very muddled flower of soft rose-pink with apricot shadings. Also included in this group are the lovely shiny-leaved 'Albéric Barbier', which is creamy white with pale yellow tonings at the centre; 'Emily Gray', fragrant, lightly double and soft yellow; and 'Jersey Beauty', a pale lemon single. These all have excellent foliage and are good as cover roses. Of course, if you really want to hide a small building or fence completely, the two Wichuraiana roadside ramblers 'Dorothy Perkins' and 'Excelsa' will suit perfectly, although they can be invasive.

Another of the very vigorous growers that does well on buildings and through tall trees and is also tolerant of a shady site is 'Cécile Brunner'. Everyone's favourite, it will grow easily to 9 m. It can be taken up 2 or 3 m and then trained along, so that when it is flowering it provides a pink lace fringe along a building.

Finally, two roses that will hide anything, no matter how unsightly the shed, fence or tankstand, are 'Seagull' and 'Rambling Rector'. Both have huge clusters of semi-double small white flowers and ample foliage, are shade-tolerant, and while 'Rambling Rector' will grow easily to 8 m, 'Seagull' will grow to at least 10 m.

'Wedding Day' growing on a tennis-court fence; 'Albéric Barbier' is used on the far side

'Paul Transon'

'François Juranville'

CHAPTER 8

For hedges

'Here tulips bloom as they are told;
Unkempt about those hedges blows
An English unofficial rose.'

Rupert Brooke

Two favourite roses conjure up a picture of English country hedges: *R. arvensis* and *R. eglanteria*. *Arvensis* will sprawl through a hedge of other plants and send out long thin trailing branches of single white flowers with light gold stamens — a very wild but graceful rose. Eglantine or Sweet Briar has small pink flowers that sit gracefully on tall, upright, sparsely foliaged plants and is one of the prettiest of all roses.

A hedge is normally planted to provide a barrier around a garden or between different areas within the garden. If you want an evergreen hedge to stop people from seeing in, there is only one rose that will do this well: *R. bracteata*, the Macartney Rose, named after Lord Macartney, who brought it back from China to England in 1793. This rose was introduced to Australia in the early nineteenth century and it is there, around a two-acre country garden, that I saw it used as the most wonderful rose hedge. Neatly clipped to 3 m high, and then arched over gateways and crenellated at the corners, it looked sturdy and impressive on a hot summer day, with its lush shiny deep green foliage. As the hedge was obviously always kept trimmed, neat and tidy, it had none of its ornamental single pure white flowers with bright yellow stamens, but if it were allowed to become a bit unruly, these would appear all through the summer.

There are two other roses which are almost evergreen, losing their leaves as the new ones appear; trained on wires, they make great hedges. 'Mermaid', a seedling of *R. bracteata*, is the best of these. It is the rose that is recommended, along with its parent, to people who desperately need to keep the neighbour's children out of their garden — the thorns on both are quite

88

savage. 'Mermaid' has large fragrant single flowers of soft butter-yellow, fading to pale cream; it needs to be only lightly pruned to keep it flowering continuously. It has the added advantage of beautiful bronze and green foliage giving a changing tonal effect. *R. laevigata*, commonly known as the Cherokee Rose, also performs well as a hedge but needs a sunny position to flower well. One of the most graceful of all roses, the large single white flowers with bright gold stamens appear to float through the hedge. It has shiny smooth green foliage and nasty thorns.

The Hybrid Musks make wonderful billowing hedges, and 'Moonlight' is probably the best of the whites. Small semi-double off-white flowers with gold stamens come in large clusters, and with studious dead-heading it is continuously in flower. Its ample reddish foliage makes it attractive for hedges, setting off the flowers very well. 'Ballerina' is a small single pink Musk that absolutely smothers the plant with its dainty roses and is very aptly named. With a similar growth habit to 'Moonlight', they go very well together — a ballerina dancing in the moonlight!

'Felicia' and 'Francesca' are two other Hybrid Musks which make fine hedge plants. With their more upright growth pattern, they form a tidier hedge. 'Felicia' has double flowers of apricot-pink and 'Francesca' lightly double apricot-lemon, so they mix together well in a hedge. 'Wilhelm' is a continuously flowering, lightly double dark red Musk with upright growth to 2 m. Mixed with the white-flowered 'Pax', it creates a very startling and

Wild roses in a country roadside hedge

89

'Bloomfield Abundance'   'Felicia'

colourful hedge. 'Pax' tends to be more lax in growth than 'Wilhelm', so the white flowers appear to float among the red. For a hedge that is softer in tone, you could use 'Felicia' instead of 'Wilhelm' with 'Pax'.

Two of David Austin's English Roses that make tall hedges are 'Red Coat' and its pretty sport 'Dapple Dawn'. These two roses are identical except for colour; 'Red Coat' is the colour of soldiers' uniforms, and 'Dapple Dawn' is a warmish mid-pink. These almost-single roses flower continuously in a frost-free climate and are best described by David Austin himself: 'The whole effect is as though a multitude of butterflies has descended upon the bushes!' They grow easily to a height of 2 m in a favourable climate and are also admirable for use at the back of a border where a continuous splash of colour is needed.

A good rose for a tall hedge is 'Bloomfield Abundance', which has perfect miniature blooms of soft pink. It is often mistaken for, and sold as, the climbing form of 'Cécile Brunner'. These two roses are superficially ident-ical, except that 'Bloomfield Abundance' has long sepals which extend beyond the bud, adding an extra dimension to the flower. 'Bloomfield Abundance' will reach a height of 2.5–3 metres, with large fern-like branches covered in sprays of flowers. It is actually sold in America as 'Spray Cécile Brunner'. Because of its upright growth it makes an ideal hedge.

For a small hedge, two of my favourites are the utilitarian Portlands 'Comte de Chambord' and 'Jacques Cartier'. They both carry a good perfume and are very good flowerers, 'Comte de Chambord' being the better of the two. Both have double rosy pink flowers displayed well against large dull green leaves. The abundant foliage helps make them great little hedging plants, growing to about 1 m.

R. *rugosa*, that useful rose from Japan and nearby countries, is perhaps one of the most popular roses for hedges. Its hybrids are generally upright in growth to about 1.5–2 m. Very thorny, they have warm green crinkled leathery foliage, which, in cool climates, has many autumn tones. R. *rugosa* and most of its hybrids are continuous-flowering or very recurrent, and the single varieties generally have large hips. The double-flowered 'Agnes' was, until recently, the only yellow Rugosa hybrid and it makes a good thick hedge, as does the smaller-growing pale pink double 'Martin Frobisher'.

My favourite of all the Rugosa hybrids is 'Blanc Double de Coubert' — that pure white loosely double beauty with dull golden stamens. Mixed with 'Hansa', a double cerise-red Rugosa, a hedge of the two becomes a statement of contrast in colour. The three small-flowered Rugosas with their carnation-shaped blooms make very floriferous hedges; 'F. J. Grootendorst' and its pink sport, which itself sported a white form, flower continuously on 1.5 m high dense shrubs. These three varieties intermingled can give a graded effect of colour. For a hedge with wonderful hips, to give the fieldmice one of their favourite delicacies, some of the single Rugosas like R. *rugosa alba* or 'Scabrosa' are ideal.

Two of the loveliest Albas, the double creamy white 'Mme Plantier' and

Roadside hedge

91

'Mme Legras de St Germain', can be clipped to good tight hedges. Both are tolerant of shade, almost totally thornless and have a strong scent. 'Mme Plantier' inevitably draws comment when displaying its flowers against plentiful rich green foliage. 'Chloris', the palest of pink double Albas, shows its flowers off against sea-green foliage and can be used in the same manner as the two previously mentioned roses.

Ever popular, but not really one of my favourites, is the not-so-old white Floribunda 'Iceberg'. A hedge of this behind a low hedge of *Lavandula dentata* is quite spectacular. It has an exceptionally long flowering season, with smallish pretty white buds often tinted with the palest pink, although opening to a rather ordinary flower.

'Iceberg'

'Pink Grootendorst'

OTHER ROSES FOR HEDGES	
'Abbotswood'	'Gruss an Aachen'
'Adam Messerich'	'Henry Hudson'
'Arthur de Sansal'	'La Reine Victoria'
'Belle Poitevine'	'Louise Odier'
'Bleu de Vibert'	'Mme Knorr'
'Calocarpa'	'Mrs R. M. Finch'
'Cardinal Hume'	'Nevada'
'Charles Albanel'	'Pearl Drift'
'Conchita'	'Portland Rose'
'Fellemberg'	'Prospero'
'Gloire Lyonnaise'	'Semi-plena'
'Golden Wings'	'Stanwell Perpetual'

CHAPTER 9

For woodland and water

'About the woodlands I will go
To see the cherry hung with snow.'
A. E. Housman

We have an English native woodland 'wild cherry', *Prunus avium*, growing at Roseneath. Although it has only very tiny cherries in our warm climate, the birds love them and transport the seed all around the garden. In a small woodland area we have this cherry hung with 'Donna Maria', an old French rambler that has great clusters of sweetly scented double white flowers. This rose does indeed give the effect of a cherry hung with the clean whiteness of fresh snow.

Tender loving care is the key to growing roses in a woodland area. They are, in general, sun lovers and those recommended for shady areas will almost always perform better in the sun. Roses grown in a woodland area where trees and shrubs have leached the soil of most nutrients must be constantly mulched with the best organic compost, they must be fed regularly and watered well. The woodland area is not a happy habitat for most roses, but if you only have a woodland garden and you want to grow roses, no problem is insurmountable.

The charm of the woodland area is in its informality, so shrub and species roses are much more appropriate than Hybrid Teas and Floribundas. Also roses on their own rootstock form much more naturally shaped shrubs for these shaded areas.

Because of their hardiness, Rugosas are one of the most favoured for this habitat. They are also among the most rewarding roses because of their attractive foliage and autumn colour. 'Thusnelda', an 1886 hybrid, produces the blowziest of soft pink blooms, but its display cannot compare with that of 'White Grootendorst', with its clusters of small carnation-shaped flowers. *R. rugosa alba* has lovely single flowers followed by orange hips. 'Calocarpa',

'Stanwell Perpetual'

R. filipes seedling

94

with its single cerise-red flowers, also produces masses of hips, and the species *R. sweginzowii* has single mid-pink flowers and very attractive vase-shaped hips. 'Roseraie de l'Hay', a rather loose double bloom of cerise-mauve, has an aromatic scent, and after the silver-pink single 'Frau Dagmar Hastrup', is one of the most popular of all Rugosas.

'Schoener's Nutkana' does well in woodland as it is quite a sturdy plant, growing to 2 m. Large single flowers of an almost lavender-pink are well set off against its greyish leaves. Foliage is important when considering a woodland area, and the Threepenny-bit Rose, *R. farreri persetosa*, with its ferny leaves, is excellent as a contrast, the silvery reddish green leaves turning to a burgundy-red in autumn. It is called the Threepenny-bit Rose because of its insignificant lavender-pink flowers.

'Dunwich Rose' makes a wonderful ground-cover under trees, with its warm green fern-like foliage. It sends out long 1.5 m branches that shoot along the ground, and this new growth is covered with small thorns, red and clear, which glow like jewels as they catch the sunlight. In rich loose soil 'Dunwich Rose' will reach about a metre. Another taller (1.5 m) variety in the *pimpinellifolia* family or group is the continuously flowering 'Stanwell Perpetual', which in warmer climates produces its very double blooms, the palest of pink, on into the winter. Although rather thorny and with foliage that often looks rusty, this scraggy-looking plant is still a great favourite, for when it produces its fresh glaucous fern-like foliage offset by its beautiful flowers, it is really splendid, particularly when catching the dappled sunlight of a woodland area.

Another even taller-growing (3.5 m) variety is 'Frühlingsanfang'. There are several of these *pimpinellifolia* roses that start their name with 'Frühlings' or 'Spring': 'Frühlingsanfang' ('Spring Beginning'), 'Frühlingsmorgen' ('Spring Morning'), 'Frühlingsduft' ('Spring Scent'), and 'Frühlingsgold' ('Spring Gold'). 'Frühlingsanfang' is the largest growing of all these, with graceful flowers, white and single on long arching branches. 'Frühlingsduft' has lovely largish blooms, double and of palest butter-yellow, blushed pink and oozing with a heavy perfume. It has long arching branches with warm green foliage. 'Frühlingsgold', with its very pretty, rich lemon single flowers, and 'Frühlingsmorgen', with its strong rose-pink single blooms, both grow to 2 m. All these roses are also suitable for hedging in shady areas.

The informality and shade-tolerance of the Hybrid Musks also make them very satisfactory roses to grow in woodland gardens. 'Bloomfield Dainty', with its recurrent-flowering single palest lemon clusters on upright but arching branches, is great for a soft contrast of colour. For something sharp and colourful, 'Wilhelm' is a bright wine-red; it sets off the rich foliage of a woodland area well and is a very prolific flowerer. 'Sadler's Wells' is a newer Hybrid Musk. Although it does well in shade, its clusters of bright red almost-single flowers are particularly attractive in dappled sunlight, where they sparkle like rubies as the light catches them. One of the most beautiful

'Lucetta'

Musks is 'Andenken an Alma de l'Aigle', a loose large round flower of soft satin-pink with a very soft apricot tone. Clusters of these pretty and very fragrant flowers are produced on a large sprawling plant.

One of David Austin's roses, 'Lucetta', is a truly graceful rose of very soft pink, with large saucer-shaped, loosely double blooms of great charm. A sprawling shrub in shade, it can also be used as a small climber, growing to 2.5 m in warm climates.

Some of the more modern shrub roses are suitable for both the woodland and the cottage garden, where they enjoy either sun or shade, or both. 'Cocktail' is a real startler. Glowing bright red with an orange tinge and a yellow centre, it is small and single in clusters. Planted in a dense shrubbery, it sends out shoots of rich reddish green foliage which bear the clusters of flowers on their ends. The heads of flowers look great as they emerge from a mixed planting of perennials and shrubs. 'Cardinal Hume', with its clusters of small double rich purple and peculiarly perfumed flowers, also looks impressive in a similar situation.

Many of the older types of climbing roses are suitable for growing into trees in a woodland. Remember to plant 1 m from the tree, in a big hole with lots of compost, then feed and water regularly. Remember also that climbing roses which are tolerant of shade will flower better when they hang out the sunny side of a tree, and that is generally where they will head.

'Dortmund' makes a good small climber (to 3 m) for a woodland fence. Large and bright rich red with a white eye, the flowers are very lush against its rich glossy green leaves. 'Karlsruhe' also does well on a fence in the woodland, with its large flowers of strong rose-pink appearing in great clusters, very frequently. Two excellent but bigger climbers for the woodland come from the German breeder Kordes. 'Parkdirektor Riggers' has clusters of flowers that are almost single and are strong bright red, a colour that can be hard to accommodate but looks good when near reddish or rich green foliage. It flowers for months on end and the flowers last for many days. 'Leverkusen' has double butter-yellow blooms well set off by shiny warm green leaves. It will grow to 4 or 5 m but should be positioned carefully because of its angular growth habit. These roses are excellent for woodland areas as they are more shade-tolerant than most climbers.

'Mme Alfred Carrière'

'Goldfinch'

'Leverkusen'

R. gentiliana and 'Ballerina'

For a rose to send way up high into trees, I would recommend one of my favourites, the graceful *R. gentiliana*, which will amble through a tree to 8 m or so, trailing its branches and dotting the tree with flushes of single white flowers blushed with very faint tinges of pink.

Many of the climbers mentioned elsewhere also do well in a woodland situation — for example, the Noisettes 'Lamarque', with its large double creamy white and very fragrant blooms, and the softer-looking white 'Mme Alfred Carrière'. Although many Noisettes are recommended for use in shade, they prefer at least dappled sun. The tea-scented 'Mrs Herbert Stevens' grows well in trees, as will 'Albéric Barbier', with its creamy white flowers, but this may tend to take a tree over with its abundance of rich green foliage.

Many people like yellow in the woodland to offset the many different greens. 'Mermaid' growing well through a stand of trees creates a sight of pure beauty. Trailing out of tall pine trees, in full flower, with the scent of the pine and 'Mermaid' mixed together, the effect is invigorating and delicious. 'Shower of Gold', with its golden muddled blooms, also looks good in a tall tree. The roses appear to be flowing down the canes as they blow in the wind, like the earlier-flowering 'Goldfinch', which is paler in colour and looser in form. 'Goldfinch' flowers very early in the spring and is a good rose with which to introduce spring colour into the garden.

One rose that will take over the woodland area and actually form a canopy over it is 'Claire Jacquier'. At Roseneath it grows 3 m up a post and at least 5 m into trees, and at its peak in late spring, with its large clusters of yellowish cream flowers, it is a sensation. An advantage is that it is almost thornless.

Roses growing beside water and reflected in it will help to create a stillness and calmness about the garden. If you have the space and a very large pond, *R. filipes* 'Kiftsgate' is magnificent; it goes everywhere, up into trees, over walls and fences, up the house, and then trails along the ground. It is best in a very large tree in a woodland beside a pond as it tolerates shade really well and looks so spectacular when trailing into the water. Very highly perfumed, with a scent that catches the air, the huge clusters of flowers seem to foam from the tree, followed in autumn by masses of smallish red hips.

'Paul's Himalayan Musk' is another informal-looking rose that does well beside water. Its clusters of buds and double pinkish mauve flowers hang down to catch reflections. *R. helenae*, with its small perfumed flowers hanging in very long clusters, seems to dance on the water. The flowers are followed by trailing bracts of tiny red hips.

'The Garland' is a very beautiful small-flowered rose that grows well in shady areas and is useful near water. It has masses of small creamy white flowers similar to, but bigger than, *Achillea* 'The Pearl'. It is great for trailing through shrubbery by water, where it surprises with its reflections.

Although not often used in this way, the Albas look good growing beside water because of their matt silver-green-grey foliage and white, often pink-tinged flowers. Two of the most superior are 'Mme Plantier' and 'Mme Legras de St Germain'. With many petals and almost quartered, 'Mme Plantier' has a button eye, and although lax in growth, can be used as a small climber. On a

Rugosas planted by a lake in a large country garden

fence and trailing over water, reflecting its perfect blossom, it is one of the best. 'Mme Legras de St Germain' is another rose that needs a fence or a trellis, and if planted by the water the reflection is superb. David Austin's 'Fair Bianca' — a cupped, full-petalled, continuous-blooming white flower with a button eye — is also sensational when used in this manner.

'Wedding Day'

'Paul's Himalayan Musk'

OTHER ROSES FOR
WOODLAND & WATER

R. x *dupontii*	'Francis E. Lester'
R. x *paulii*	'Fred Streeter'
'Aglaia'	'Geranium'
'Agnes'	'Hansa'
'Anaïs Ségales'	'Hebe's Lip'
'Anne Endt'	'Henry Hudson'
'Apple Blossom'	'Kathleen'
'Autumnalis'	'Milky Way'
'Belle Amour'	'Moonlight'
'Belle Poitevine'	'Nevada'
'Bobbie James'	'Parade'
'Chloris'	'Semi-plena'
'Dr. W. van Fleet'	'Wedding Day'

CHAPTER 10

For containers and ground-cover

'Water your damned flower-pots, do!'
Robert Browning

Browning's is the soundest advice that could be given to a gardener who grows roses in pots or containers. Although roses hate wet feet, they love to be watered — a couple of hot summer days without water will have them drooping and stressed.

Container-grown roses are useful anywhere — patios, verandahs, balconies, small gardens and as features in large gardens. After seeing thirteen steps with twenty-six pots of alternating red and white Polyantha Roses flowering all summer in a large Mediterranean-style garden overlooking the sea through tall cypress trees, I would never hesitate to recommend the use of containers in large gardens. Standard roses in pots on either side of a front entrance can be a very attractive feature, or a single standard can look good as a centrepiece in a grouping of containers. Several containers can become the focal point on a large terrace or patio area, with procumbent roses spilling from pots at the front, small-growing roses behind these, and then perhaps a standard rose at the back. Similar-toned roses can create a quiet area of colour, or contrasting colours can be combined for a more glittering display. Containers can be used to define paths or as a focal point in a garden. Container-grown roses can add interest when placed either side of a garden seat, at the corner of a building or beside a garden pond. There are infinite possibilities for using potted roses in small townhouse gardens, large country gardens and anything between.

Growing roses in pots is like growing them in the garden — with love, care and attention they will perform well. Plastic pots are best, although not

Pots of 'Green Ice' frame the steps leading to the front
door of this house (Gil Hanly)

the most attractive. If you are using pottery or terracotta containers that are
unglazed, it is a good idea to line the sides with plastic. All containers need
good drainage, so a reasonable layer of stones or pieces of broken pot is
needed at the bottom. A couple of good handfuls of charcoal should be mixed
in with this to absorb manure residues, or salt residues that leach from the
pots. Do not use a straight potting mix but include approximately half soil
with the potting mix or peat as roses prefer a heavier mixture. The pot should
never be smaller than bucket size — the bigger the pot, the better, except for
very small-growing roses like 'Rouletii' and 'Perla de Montserrat', and
modern miniatures. Use small pots for small plants and larger pots for bigger
plants for a balanced effect.

A slow-release fertiliser like long-term Osmocote, Nutracote or Magamp
may be added to the mixture at the recommended rate. It is vital to pay
careful attention to watering: during the summer and dry periods plants will
need to be watered every one or two days; in the winter there is probably no
need to water at all unless the plants are under cover, and then it may be
necessary to water once a week. It is better to water the surface of the soil, not
the plant itself; just occasionally give the plant a good wash.

Every three years, in winter, repot the plant, using new potting mix.
Wash all the old mix off and clip the roots back, taking out any dead roots and
cutting others back to about 15 cm from the base of the plant.

Few roses are suitable for window boxes and hanging baskets, other than
the very small-growing roses like 'Rouletii' and 'Perla de Montserrat', as there

is not sufficient soil in these types of containers. 'Rouletii', said to be the first of the modern miniatures, was found in Switzerland by a Major Roulet in 1918. It has small dark pink flowers, no bigger than a fingernail, on tiny plants no more than 26 cm high. The perfectly shaped little buds and flowers are held upright and display themselves continuously all season. It is a good little plant for mixing with herbs in a window box, where it is said to have been discovered. 'Rouletii' was crossed with 'Cécile Brunner' to make the softer pink 'Perla de Montserrat'. Another seedling of 'Cécile Brunner' is the enchanting 'Grandchild'. Growing to 60 cm, it has small rose-pink flowers that are darker at the centre and quite tight in shape, more so than the quickly blown bud of 'Cécile Brunner'. This rose was bred in New Zealand and deserves wider recognition.

Many of the procumbent and other smaller-growing roses do well in containers because they have smaller root systems than large bush and shrub roses and they flower constantly. The more procumbent will spill out of the container in a very attractive manner. The Polyantha Roses are some of the most suitable for containers because they are generally more compact in growth and very free-flowering. The small pink double-flowered 'The Fairy' is the most popular of all. 'Pride of Hurst', with its pretty soft salmon rosettes, and 'Katharina Zeimet', with its white rosettes, are varieties which, like all Polyanthas, are constantly in flower. The loosely flowered red 'Gloria Mundi' and similar-shaped warm pink 'Cameo' look particularly good in terracotta pots. 'Anna Maria de Montravel', a great little white rose, and the palest pink 'Mignonette' are the oldest of all Polyanthas, both having been produced in France in 1880. A welcome member of this class of roses is the New Zealand-raised 'Mrs Merrilees', which has flowers that are almost a tiny form of 'Ballerina', being single, pink with a white eye, and held upright in

'Grandchild'   'Popcorn', a seedling from 'Katharina Zeimet'

103

'Mrs Merrilees' growing in a pot with 'Bantry
Bay' on the trellis above (Gil Hanly)

clusters on an upright-growing plant to 60 cm. Another single rosy pink with a
paler centre is the continuous-flowering 'Tapis Volant'. It has small orange-
red hips on a 60 cm high plant that sprawls out to 1.2 m.

'Sneprincesse', 'Muttertag' and 'Vatertag', sometimes known as Paree
Roses, are excellent in terracotta pots because of their colours and their
continuous-flowering habit. 'Sneprincesse' has globular buds opening pure
white and cupped. 'Muttertag' ('Mothers' Day') is the same but a blood-red,
and 'Vatertag' ('Fathers' Day') is a strong salmon-orange sport of 'Muttertag'.
These roses have very glossy green foliage and grow to small compact plants
of about 60 cm.

Many of the continuous-flowering Teas and Hybrid Teas that are superb
garden roses also perform well in pots, as long as they are well watered and
kept well drained. Three of the beautiful larger single hybrids are truly
elegant roses: the strawberry-pink 'Dainty Bess'; its cream seedling with
frilled pink edges to the petals, 'Ellen Willmott'; and 'White Wings', also a
single 'Dainty Bess' seedling with larger pure white satin petals which are
floppier in habit than the other two. These roses are quite erect in growth and
are suitable for pots where you need height rather than width at the base.

One of the most beautiful of all Hybrid Teas is 'Ophelia', which has well-shaped buds that open a very pale pink. This rose sported the slightly darker 'Mme Butterfly', which sported the warmer-coloured 'Lady Sylvia'. These three roses growing in separate pots but grouped together are ideal for a small terrace or patio garden, and they are all picking roses. Of the older Teas, 'Triomphe de Luxembourg', with its large round soft salmon-pink blooms, 'Rosette de Lizzy', a big and many-petalled rose, yellow fused with pink and deeper tonings, and the lavender-pink 'Catherine Mermet', with its pointed buds, are good container plants.

Many of the Hybrid Musks can be grown in containers as large shrubs or staked on pillars to give height. 'Mozart', a small single red, 'Thisbe', a semi-double buff, 'Robin Hood', single and a sharp red, 'Pink Prosperity', very double and warm pink, and 'Francesca', a loosely double pale buff-yellow, are winners in warmer climates. The most successful, though, grown as a climber and carefully espaliered on a wall, is the small-flowered semi-double white 'Moonlight'. I once saw this rose, along with 'Cocktail' — a single orange-crimson with a yellow eye — growing in an old stone trough against a pale brick wall, and it made one of the most attractive courtyard plantings that I have seen.

It is difficult to draw the line between modern roses and old roses, for although some roses are recently bred, they inherit their shape and style from old-fashioned roses. These include some of the modern shrub roses suitable

'Pink Bells' growing in a pot with other roses over an archway

for containers, like 'Elmshorn', whose clusters of small double cherry-pink flowers last for days. Being lax in growth, it makes a good small climber, as does the more erect-growing 'Fred Loads', which has glowing soft salmon-orange semi-double flowers. 'Fred Loads' and 'Radway Sunrise' make perfect companions; 'Radway Sunrise', a soft salmon colour darkening with age, is mixed with yellow and rose pink — a single flower with great brilliance. When planted in containers these roses need support. They can be placed in front of a trellis or wall on which they will climb, or be tied to a 2 m stake.

For the real old-rose enthusiasts who need to grow their roses in pots, the Damasks 'Gloire de Guilan', 'Omar Khayyám', 'St Nicholas' and 'Mme Zoetmans', along with the Gallicas 'Belle de Crécy', 'Duchesse d'Angoulême', 'Tricolore de Flandre', and the Moss Roses 'Little Gem', 'Général Kléber', 'Mme Louis Lévêque' and 'Nuits de Young', are all very valid choices.

'Gloire de Guilan' can be used as a dense shrub, growing to over 1.2 m. It is pale pink and very fragrant, as is 'Omar Khayyám', which is one of the smaller-growing Damasks. Double and soft pink, it is said to have been grown from seed that came from Omar Khayyám's tomb. 'St Nicholas' is also reasonably small in growth and is a good container plant for the small garden. Semi-double and warm pink, it also has a fine display of hips. 'Mme Zoetmans' has quartered flowers of softest pink fading to pinkish white and a very upright growth habit; hedges of this grown in individual pots can be well used in the division of a small area.

'Tricolore de Flandre' is the best of the striped roses to be grown in a container. Nicely perfumed, double and very soft pink and purple striped, it is erect in growth, which is a real plus for massed containers. 'Belle de Crécy'

'Raubritter' is a perfect ground-cover rose

106

'Mme Louis Lévêque'

and the 'Duchesse d'Angoulême' are even more upright in growth and are two of the loveliest of this type. The 'Duchesse' is loosely double and very pale pink, darker on opening, whereas the quartered flowers of 'Belle de Crécy' are warmer in colour, with tinges of greyish violet.

Some Moss Roses are quite compact, making them suitable for containers. They generally recur well in warmer climates but really prefer a colder frosty winter. 'Little Gem', with its smallish round red flowers, is probably the lowest-growing of all the Mosses. It is quite the opposite of the more sprawling 'Général Kléber', which has sparkling blooms of glowing satin-pink, muddled and loosely double. This rose needs plenty of room, covering an area of at least 1.5 m wide and high. 'Mme Louis Lévêque' also deserves very strong recommendation; muddled and double, a glowing soft powder-pink with very lush flowers, it is truly one of the most attractive of all the Moss Roses. Another Moss, and one that is a great favourite, is 'Nuits de Young'. It has black-red buds that open to small purple-red flowers with a heady perfume. A good container plant, it is erect in growth and does not take up much space.

Ground-cover roses are simply roses that will cover an area of ground. Any shrub that is lax or spreading and covers a wide area, no matter how tall, could be called a ground-cover. The roses included here are the more procumbent and trailing varieties that are suitable for growing in containers but can also be used as ground-covers or foaming over banks and walls. Most of the smaller-

'St Nicholas'

'Lavender Dream'

growing procumbent roses are modern, but with their small single or rosette-type flowers, they fit well into gardens where old-fashioned roses are used.

'Snow Carpet', with its small creamy white rosettes, is one of the lowest-growing roses, spreading out to 1.2 m. It has very small dense foliage and makes a good ground-hugging mat 10–15 cm high. The small single pink 'Nozomi' also makes a low-growing mat, spreading to 2.5 m. 'Akashi', which has small rose-pink rosettes and a growth habit similar to 'Snow Carpet', has the added advantage of being almost thornless. Slightly higher growing but still very procumbent is 'Swany', which has pretty small double white flowers that are produced continuously. People often complain that they can never weed underneath these roses, but there is an easy way. Just slide a rake handle along the ground under the trailing branches and lift them, then hoe or weed underneath.

For a rose that will trail 2 m or more, 'Sea Foam' is a winner, repeatedly producing masses of clusters of medium-sized off-white blooms with a pink blush. It is a very adaptable rose and can be used in containers, as a ground-cover, a sprawling shrub or small climber.

Some of the older ramblers can be used as procumbent ground-covers and will cover the ground for up to 5 m. 'Paul Transon' is one of the best of these; with flowers that are raggy and double in form, a warm salmon-pink, it will send out long trailers that create a dense and sprawling plant. 'François Juranville', with flowers that are very similar but a much paler salmon-pink, has the same habit and works well when sprawled over a bank. If you want to smother a bank completely, don't forget the pink double cluster-flowered 'Dorothy Perkins', or the red type of this rose, 'Excelsa'.

One of the best ground-covers is the almost-evergreen cream double-flowered 'Albéric Barbier'. This rambler will densely coat the ground with its lush dark green foliage for 5–6 m. Most unusual is the white single raggy-looking rose *R. x paulii*, which is very special and one of my favourites. It is believed to be an unusual mixture of the two species *R. arvensis*, the English Field Rose, and *R. rugosa*, and hails from Asia. Although very low-growing and a good ground-cover, it is best put on a fence out of harm's way because it has very sharp thorns.

Three shrub roses which are sprawling in growth and make taller ground-covers are 'Lavender Dream', 'Yesterday' and 'Marjorie Fair'. 'Lavender Dream' grows to 1 m high and wide, and should really be called 'Lilac Dream' for it has soft lilac flowers which create a great sheet of colour. It is very popular with cottage garden enthusiasts, as is 'Yesterday', which is more reddish lilac in colour and is very similar in growth habit; both are lightly semi-double. 'Marjorie Fair', which has single flowers of bright red with a white eye, is quite strong in colour, making it harder to place in the garden. This rose has a more spreading habit than 'Lavender Dream'.

'Mme Plantier'

OTHER ROSES FOR
CONTAINERS & GROUND-COVER

'Achievement'	'Eva'	'Mrs R. M. Finch'
'Anna Oliver'	'Fairyland'	'Nancy Steen'
'Bredon'	'Felicia'	'Nightfall'
'Céline Forestier'	'Golden Showers'	'Paul Crampel'
'Conchita'	'Gruss an Aachen'	'Pinkie' (bush)
'Dainty Maid'	'Hermosa'	'Pinkie' (climbing)
'Danaë'	'Mme Knorr'	'Sanders' White'
'Rose de Meaux'	'Marie Parvie'	'Sparkler'

CHAPTER 11

For hips

'I see a lily on thy brow,
With anguish moist and fever dew;
And on thy cheek a fading rose
Fast withereth too.'

John Keats

Rose hips not only provide larger amounts of vitamin C than oranges or lemons, they also have vitamins A, B, E and P. Taking a cup of rose-hip tea daily is good for cleansing the kidneys and gallbladder, and acts as a diuretic. If Keats had known all this, perhaps his lady's cheek would not have lost its bloom!

The large cherry-shaped hips of the single-flowered Rugosas draw most comment in the garden. They glow with a bright waxy sheen in deep orange-reds, attracting not only the eye of the human visitor to the garden but also that of the small and cheeky fieldmouse. Although mice do not like the furry seeds inside the hip, they are quite happy to nibble away on the juicy flesh, leaving the bush very untidy, with half-eaten hips and seed spread everywhere.

A seedling plant of *R. rugosa* 'Typica' at Roseneath has the largest hips of any of this species that I have ever seen. The plant itself grows to 1.5 m and covers an area over 2 m square. Large single flowers of a satin cerise-pink are produced all summer through, so from mid-summer there are always hips on the plant.

Other single Rugosas that are well worth growing, not only for their hips but also for their flowers and foliage, include 'Frau Dagmar Hastrup', a soft satin silver-pink of great beauty. It grows to 1.5 m but is inclined to spread like a ground-cover in its early days of growth. 'Scabrosa' is another Rugosa that has big round hips. It has very brilliant rosy cerise single flowers that repeat constantly through the seasons.

110

For sheer quantity of hips, 'Calocarpa' is remarkable. A cross between *R. rugosa* and *R. chinensis*, its single reddish pink flowers smother the tall (2 m) plant, followed by a profusion of red hips. Recently bred by Hazel Le Rougetel is the single lavender-pink 'Corylus', which has masses of round cherry-red hips. This rose has finer foliage than most Rugosas, a rich and shiny warm green, which, with its lightly arching branches, makes it a beautiful specimen plant.

Although most of the single-flowered Rugosas produce the best hips, some of the double-flowered hybrids bear good hips as well: 'Hansa' has a large loosely double purple-cerise flower with furled petals and produces great hips, as do the soft lilac-pink 'Belle Poitevine' and the light red 'Charles Albanel', one of the lower-growing Rugosas.

Before leaving the Rugosas and their marvellous hips, we should mention a New Zealand rose, 'Anne Endt', an *R. foliolosa* Rugosa hybrid. Growing to a height of 1.8 m, this sprawling shrub has a more fern-like quality to its leaves than the other Rugosas. The single-petalled flowers are of rich magenta with golden stamens, and they set deep red hips, smaller than most Rugosas. A lovely sprawling but graceful rose, it is well worth growing, but beware — it will sucker for miles, so always choose a budded plant.

Another invasive but truly wonderful hip-producing rose is *R. pimpinellifolia* (previously *spinosissima*), the Scotch Briar or Burnet Rose. Flowering very early in the season, this delicate single cream rose has fern-like foliage and a multitude of prickles. There are many Burnet Roses, double forms and hybrids of the species, and two that we grow are known today as 'Double Cream' and 'Double Pink', the colour of the 'Double Pink' springing from the pink tinges found in the single form. After producing many

'Penelope' with hips   'Calocarpa'

'Anne Endt'   'Wedding Day'

flowers early in the season, it leaves a great sprinkling of small rich black hips that have a slight reddish hue; if they had a bluish hue they could easily be mistaken for blueberries. If you have light loam, be careful where you plant these as they can take over.

A climber that receives comment for its large hips is the burnished 'Meg'. This lovely slightly double rose has apricot tones offset by its darker stamens. Although it is slightly recurrent, the first large flowers can be left on the plants to produce large globular hips of deep orange. Said to be a seedling of another favourite, 'Paul's Lemon Pillar', 'Meg' has pride of place in our garden. 'Paul's Lemon Pillar' has very large round cabbage-like flowers that are almost white, tinged with greenish lemon; when they catch the sun they sparkle. Well scented and a good picking rose, it is widely grown even though it has a very brief flowering. Like its daughter 'Meg', it has large globular hips, so large that they look heavy. Another rose in this group is 'Mme Grégoire Staechelin' or the 'Spanish Beauty'. It is interesting to note that both this and 'Paul's Lemon Pillar' have 'Frau Karl Druschki' as a parent, so it is a grandparent of 'Meg'. 'Frau Karl Druschki' is one of the most sublime of all the white roses, and in 1906 it produced a climbing sport, presumably the form used in the breeding of these roses.

Another rose with good hips that can be used as a climber is 'Fritz Nobis'. In mid-spring it is a picture, bedecked in medium-sized soft pink blooms with a hint of apricot — a very feminine rose. It is best to avoid dead-heading 'Fritz Nobis' as it produces wonderful orange hips. 'Scharlachglut', the aptly named 'Scarlet Fire', is a huge shrub with very big single flowers and is best used as a small climber. It has big vase-shaped hips of rich orange that turn rich red with age.

R. helenae   *R. moyesii*

The Synstylae roses, so called because the styles are fused to form a single protruding element in the middle of the flower, are many and varied, and often produce masses of hips. In spring *R. helenae* is covered in small single off-white flowers followed by huge clusters of up to 80 small orange-red hips. *R. multiflora* also has large clusters of red hips in great profusion; there are so many seedling varieties of this rose that it is best to strike a cutting from one that has proven itself. The charmingly named 'Rambling Rector' produces great clusters of tiny hips after its lightly double white flowers fall in spring, and it looks great hanging out of a large tree.

Rose hips are now frequently found in floral decorations. Most varieties used have vase-shaped hips, although some are globular, round or oval in shape. The roses from which these come are mostly related to the Rugosas and have fern-like foliage. They are all shrubs, although some send out magnificent long arching branches up to 3 m. One such plant is *R. sweginzowii*, which has 3 cm hips of bright tomato-red. *R. setipoda* also grows tall but instead of having well-spaced flowers they come in clusters, and the hips are in tight groups of up to sixteen. These hips have tiny, tiny thorns and look as if they need a shave. A large sprawling shrub which looks wonderful in a wild and overgrown garden is *R. webbiana*, with its dainty bluish ferny foliage. Pale pink small pretty flowers are followed by little vase-shaped hips.

R. moyesii and some of its twentieth-century hybrids also produce vase-shaped hips. This species is very angular in growth and can be espaliered perfectly on a fence or trellis. The hips, more an orange than a tomato colour, are produced in quantity from attractive dull crimson flowers. 'High-downensis' is a great rose for the large informal garden, with a graceful arching growth pattern and flowers that are softer in colour and hips that are

R. eglanteria over an archway

larger and much rosier in tone than the species. Other hybrids such as 'Fred Streeter', 'Sealing Wax', 'Wintoniensis', 'Geranium' and 'Nevada' also set good hips.

R. glauca is another species rose to provide a generous display of hips. After the flowers drop, it produces red hips with a violet tinge that tones beautifully with its glaucous foliage. This foliage is wonderful in arrangements with the rose 'Anaïs Ségales'.

In warmer climates the Hybrid Musks are among the most successful roses. 'Ballerina' has large heads of small pink white-centred flowers leading to large clusters of small oval red hips. With constant dead-heading, it is continuously in flower; to get a good display of hips, dead-heading should be stopped in late summer. 'Erfurt', a Hybrid Musk cross with large rich reddish pink almost-single blooms that pale to white at the centre, is also useful as a small climber to 2.5 m. It produces large orange hips, as does everyone's favourite, 'Penelope', with its lightly double creamy apricot flowers.

Often when people are selecting roses, they will not buy once-flowering varieties. This is unfortunate as many other garden plants flower only for the same short period of time. Length of flowering should be just another consideration, along with colour, shape and other attributes.

CHAPTER 12

For perfume

'What's in a name? that which we call a rose
By any other name would smell as sweet.'
William Shakespeare

Roses are very much a part of romance, and it's a great pity that red roses purchased at florists, although perfect in shape, have no perfume at all. Shakespeare would have been over the moon if he had been able to pick the blooms of 'Étoile de Holland' for Anne Hathaway. Repeat-flowering and exuding a heavy fruit-like fragrance, it remains one of the most popular of red roses. It is best to grow the climbing form of this rose, particularly over an archway through which you often walk, as the flowers hang down.

Another of the best red roses is the relatively modern Hybrid Tea 'Papa Meilland'. This 1963 rose, with petals like velvet and a very strong scent, flowers continuously. Unlike many of the red roses, it does not droop its head, making it a good cutting rose. No list of perfumed red roses could be made without mention of 'Crimson Glory'. Bred by Kordes in 1935, it has large round cabbage-like flowers of dark burgundy-red that just ooze a rich perfume. The only failing is that its blooms hang from weak stems, although this can be a bonus on the climbing form as you can then look up into its many-petalled flowers. Unfortunately, 'Crimson Glory' has passed this fault on to its offspring 'Ena Harkness', who has in turn passed it on to 'Josephine Bruce', both of which have a heady fragrance; again, the climbing forms of these are preferable if you have the space.

Many-petalled roses are the best to grow for perfume as the more petals a rose has the more perfume it exudes. One of David Austin's roses, the shrub climber 'Abraham Darby', is a good example of this. Its large pale apricot blooms with many petals exude a distinctly rose scent. Two other David Austin roses that have rich perfumes are the very double rose-pink 'Pretty Jessica', which flowers continuously on a low-growing bush, and 'Gertrude

Jekyll', which is a strong reddish pink and double — a very useful tall plant, ideal in mixed borders.

Attar of roses, the essential oil for the production of rose scents and perfumes, is distilled from the Damasks. Interestingly, the perfume is not lost when heated, unlike other perfumes. Plants of 'Trigintipetala', or the Rose of Kazanlik, have been grown by the thousand in the valleys of Bulgaria for this purpose. The flowers are loosely double and are a soft rosy pink. Together with that other beautiful soft pink Damask 'Ispahan', it is often used in the manufacture of potpourri. 'De la Grifferaie' is another potpourri rose with a strong scent, but the huge bush it forms tends to look shabby and untidy; its tightly packed double flowers of dark mauve-pink also tend to ball a bit. If you are going to grow a rose especially for potpourri, you really can't do better than the Autumn Damask, which is a very ancient rose and is like a repeat-flowering form of 'Trigintipetala'. All these old roses are still widely grown for their perfume.

One of the oldest and greatest favourites for its scent, particularly that of its leaves, is the Sweet Briar or the Eglantine Rose, *R. eglanteria*. In a warm moist spring, this rose is at its best. After a shower on a sunny day, it is one of the delights of the garden to pass this pretty soft pink single flower and inhale the Granny Smith apple scent that pervades the air around it.

'De la Grifferaie'

116

'Mme Isaac Pereire'   'Mme Ernst Calvat'

R. banksiae alba plena is strategically placed near walkways in the garden at Roseneath. A vigorous small double white rambler, it leaves its violet scent hanging in the air. Another that will deliciously perfume the garden is the modern 'Sutter's Gold'. This 1950 Hybrid Tea is yellow with an orange-red flame through it and is planted by many old rose fanatics for its perfume alone.

Bourbon Roses are great favourites and are renowned for their perfume. Although the beautiful blowzy powder-pink 'Souvenir de la Malmaison' is known as the 'Queen of Fragrance', its relative, cerise-pink 'Mme Isaac Pereire', and its paler lavender-pink sport, 'Mme Ernst Calvat', should really have that title, scoring 10 out of 10 for fragrance. Not too thorny, 'Mme Isaac' and 'Mme Ernst' can be used as large shrubs or small climbers. The only real fault with these quartered and densely petalled roses is that they ball badly in the wet, their saving grace being the quick repeat of flowers and, of course, their fragrance.

The Bourbon 'Louise Odier' is a strongly perfumed rich double pink which flowers continuously and is good espaliered on a fence as it will produce many more blooms when grown in this fashion. A mixture of 'Louise Odier' and the shyer but more erect-growing ice-white 'Boule de Neige' creates a highly fragrant and colourful combination. It must be remembered that 'Boule de Neige' is one of the Bourbons that likes a warm sunny spot and does not tolerate shade, unlike the others mentioned here.

Two other great Bourbons for perfume are the thornless 'Zéphirine Drouhin', which is a strong reddish pink, and its pale pink sport, 'Kathleen Harrop'. Both these roses are more loosely petalled than other Bourbons so they do not ball. They are ideal for those gardeners who have a lawn-mowing partner who complains about roses jumping out at them and tearing at their

'Mme Pierre Oger'

tender limbs like a terrified wild cat, a common complaint best remedied by a change of partner, not removal of the rose bushes.

Some of the smaller-growing roses with strong perfumes are the early Hybrid Teas. If you want a rose for cutting, 'Ophelia' is excellent. It is the palest of pale pinks and has sported the soft pink 'Mme Butterfly' and the medium pink 'Lady Sylvia'. Surrounded by companion plants of only the softest blue, they create a hazy fusion of colour. Although 'Anna Pavlova' is a modern rose, produced by Peter Beales, it must be mentioned here for it certainly scoffs at those who say modern roses have no fragrance. 'Anna Pavlova' has slightly globular flowers of the softest powder-pink, darker in the centre. It has a sport that is creamy white and just as fragrant, fittingly named 'Sir Frederick Ashton', as a partner for Anna Pavlova, for his eightieth birthday. All these roses have a spicy scent.

When people talk of tea-scented roses they really do mean with the aroma of Earl Grey and other teas. One of the best of these is the very beautiful 'Lady Hillingdon', which is a strong apricot-yellow, lightly double with a most delicious and fresh scent. This rose will flower continuously but, like all Teas, prefers a warm sunny sheltered spot to perform really well. 'Souvenir d'un Ami , a very double rose of rich dark pink with an almost apricot tinge, is another. 'Archiduc Joseph', which is known in New Zealand as 'Monsieur Tillier', is a very beautiful rose that is almost quartered, salmon-pink and flowers continuously. The true 'Monsieur Tillier' is lightly double and grows well as a climber in warm climates. Very early to flower, it repeats with large bursts of bright scarlet violet-tinged flowers and carries a sweet tea scent.

'Francis Dubreuil', dark red and lightly cupped, a softer and more delicate-looking flower than the red 'Crimson Glory' and its siblings, has a fruity tea scent, as has the fully double, cup-shaped, medium to soft pink 'Mme Wagram'. Bright rose-pink, and also fully double and cupped, is 'Mrs B. R. Cant', which carries a fruity tea scent that has a close affinity to raspberries.

A rose that performs particularly well in warm climates is the Hybrid Musk. The Reverend Pemberton, an early twentieth-century rose fanatic, used two descendants of *R. multiflora* and *R. moschata* ('Trier' and 'Aglaia') and crossed them with other more modern roses to give us the Pemberton Musks. Their scent is spicier than other roses, although it is quite light and floats in the air. These roses can be controlled as large sprawling bushes or left to become small climbers. 'Buff Beauty', a bronzy apricot, is one of the best of the Musks for perfume. 'Lavender Lassie' is another of the larger-flowered Musks, with very double flowers of strong lilac-pink. The bush is smothered in bloom, and you do not need to bend your head to smell the spicy perfume. As with most of the Musks, it does very well in the shade, although nearly all roses flower much better in the sun. 'Penelope' is one of the most popular of all the Musks, with its semi-double flowers of soft apricot-pink with yellow stamens. 'Eva', from Kordes, is single and cerise-red with a quite strongly spiced scent. Like most of the Musks, it flowers continuously. 'Pink Prosperity', developed by the Bentalls, who carried on Pemberton's work, also has a light spicy scent. It has soft rosy pink flowers that are medium sized and borne in clusters.

There are many other fragrant roses that are well worth growing, like the

'Buff Beauty'

'Francis Dubreuil'

'Königin von Dänemark'

Gallicas, including *R. gallica officinalis*, also known as the Red Rose of Lancaster or the Apothecary's Rose. Once-flowering, with lightly double blooms of soft pinkish red, it holds its scent right through the day. 'Anaïs Ségales' flowers very early in the season, with floppy double blooms of a purple-red, becoming slatey with age. It looks wonderful in a vase on its own and fills a room with its deep rich scent.

The Albas are also certainly worth growing for their sweet scent. The double white 'Maxima' and the many-petalled soft pink 'Félicité Parmentier' have a luscious scent. 'Chloris', which is a pale pink double, and the warmer-coloured and very double 'Königin von Dänemark' also have a sweet fragrance.

Two fragrant roses not to be left out are the tender climbers 'Lamarque' and 'Maréchal Niel'. 'Lamarque' is a multi-petalled but loose-flowered pure white rose with soft lemon buds, constantly in flower in a warm climate. 'Maréchal Niel' is one of the most fragrant of all roses, but it must be grown under cover as it balls badly in any rain. Its warm greenish butter-yellow flowers open from sharp buds to loosely petalled fully double blooms.

CHAPTER 13

For the collector's garden

'Gather ye rosebuds while ye may,
Old Time still is a-flying:
And this same flower that smiles today,
To-morrow will be dying.'
                                    Robert Herrick

There are many roses that are not found in gardens generally but are grown for their unusual habits or features such as thorns or flowers, or just for their historical associations. These are the varieties that may be included in a collector's garden, where the interest is in the plants themselves rather than the garden. Some rose collectors may decide to specialise in growing species roses, or perhaps Mosses, Gallicas or Centifolias. This chapter includes varieties which have a certain fascination for us and have therefore found their way into our garden at Roseneath.

One of the most interesting is *R. ciliata*, the Gooseberry Rose, a species from China. With dense fern-like foliage on a tall twiggy plant of 2 m, it produces single creamy flowers followed by edible but sour fruit like large orange gooseberries, hanging below the foliage. Seed was brought out of China to New Zealand by Ron Gordon, who found it growing in the rare plant area of the Kunming Gardens. It makes an ideal hedge with its very sharp small thorns, and it is used in this way at Kunming. *R. stellata* is another rose, found in western Mexico and California, that fruits like a gooseberry bush. It has single deep lavender-pink flowers and reaches a height of 2 m.

R. sericea pteracantha, also from China, has large flat thorns that, when in their young stage of growth, are like pieces of garnet glass that glow in the sunlight. The small single white flowers have only four petals, which is very unusual as single roses generally have five petals. With its long branches of up to 3.5 m, it is a singular plant as it waves its glowing thorns in the sun. It has fern-like foliage, as does *R. xanthina spontanea*, or 'Canary Bird' as it is

121

R. sericea pteracantha   *R. xanthina spontanea* or 'Canary Bird'

commonly known. This rose was brought to Europe from China in 1908. It is smothered in small single bright butter-yellow flowers (from which it gets its name) in the spring. Rather procumbent in growth, it is very tolerant of shade and does well in a woodland garden.

One of the most striking of these species roses is *R. foetida bicolor* or 'Austrian Copper', which has a bright salmon-orange small single flower. A rose that loves the sun, it looks magnificent when a 3 m high bush is smothered in flowers in mid-spring. Originating before the fifteenth century, it is a sport of *R. foetida*, the Austrian Briar, which has rich buttercup-yellow flowers. A climbing form of this variety, 'Lawrence Johnston', is a cross between *R. foetida persiana* and 'Mme Victor Verdier' and has semi-double flowers of a strong yellow.

Many plants sport new and different roses, and one of the most beautiful of these is 'Adam Rackles', which is a sport of the bush form of 'Mme Caroline Testout'. A flower that looks as if it is made of wax or satin, it is marbled and not striped, pale pink and white. We are lucky enough to have a plant at Roseneath that has reverted back to 'Mme Caroline Testout' and has both types of flowers on it. It flowers from spring to autumn on a bush that is well over 1 m high.

If you wish to include a Gallica and an Alba in your collection of roses, what better ones to choose than *R. gallica officinalis*, more commonly known as the Red Rose of Lancaster or the Apothecary's Rose, and *R.* x *alba*, the White Rose of York. The Red Rose of Lancaster is light red, loosely double and very highly perfumed. It sported one of the most popular striped roses,

R. gallica versicolor, or 'Rosa Mundi'. These are two of the oldest roses known, being found in Europe and Asia. The White Rose of York is a delicately perfumed single pure white flower that is well offset by its soft glaucous foliage, not to be confused with 'Maxima', which is a very beautiful double off-white flower, also sometimes called the White Rose of York; and to add to the confusion it is also known as the Jacobite Rose and Bonnie Prince Charlie's Rose.

While on the subject of the roses of York and Lancaster, we must mention the Damask of this name. The rose 'York and Lancaster' grows to a very scraggy 2.5 m shrub which has shaggy flowers that are loosely double. The flowers can be white or soft lavender-pink, or a mixture of the two colours, resulting in a multitude of different flowers, in clusters, covering the bush — a great talking point. Of course the Rose of Kazanlik or 'Trigintipetala' is a true collector's rose, as is 'Ispahan'. They both have a delicious perfume. The Damasks have produced the most beautiful white garden rose there is, 'Mme Hardy'. It is so refined yet magnificent, with its multitude of quilled petals that reveal a green button eye. A real charmer, it is a very vigorous grower that can be used as a climber and is tolerant of shade. Its only fault is that it is once-flowering, but it really deserves a place in any garden. David Austin has gone a long way to producing a white rose that is very double and of great beauty as well as being continuously in flower with his 1982 'Fair Bianca'. For a white rose that flowers from spring to autumn, this is the one I would choose.

The Roses of Provence are the Cabbage Roses, so called because of their many petals. *R. centifolia*, which dates from before the sixteenth century, is

'Mme Hardy'

the oldest of these. Cabbage-shaped and dark pink, it is blowzy with an aromatic perfume. A bit of a sprawler, it will easily cover an area 2 m square. Another of these roses grown for interest's sake is the Lettuce-leaf Rose, 'Bullata', named for its tough crinkled leaves. Its flowers are not unlike *R. centifolia* but are less profuse. 'Juno' is another great favourite, with its round and very full flowers of the softest off white-pink. It is the type of rose you sink your nose into and feel you could get drunk on its perfume.

Every collection of roses should have a Sweet Briar, so I have chosen 'La Belle Distinguée' to be used as a hedge. Quite tidy and erect in growth, this hybrid retains the scented leaves of the Eglantine Rose. It produces masses of double red flowers in late spring and early summer, and will form a huge plant of 2 m or so. Interspersed with several plants of *R. eglanteria*, it makes a wonderful hedge.

Of the Portland Roses, 'Rose de Rescht' is one of the most fascinating: an unusual red with mauve tints, the small flowers have a strong perfume. It is a compact plant for that small place near the end of a shrubbery; another plus is that it does well in woodland and is shade-tolerant. 'Mme Knorr' makes a good small hedging plant, with its lightly double flowers of warm pink. There is nothing better than a strongly perfumed rose like this used as a hedge plant for the perfume will pervade a great area.

R. pimpinellifolia, or the Scotch Rose, makes wonderful ground-cover mounds in an informal garden. Although it tends to spread, it can easily be kept under control. The foliage is fern-like and will trail along the ground for 2 m. Small single cream flowers give way to little blackcurrant-shaped hips. There are several forms of the Scotch Rose: 'Dunwich Rose' has creamy yellow single flowers; 'Golden Wings' is a newer variety which flowers

'La Belle Distinguée'

124

R. roxburghii, the Chestnut Rose, with its chestnut-like hip

continuously with larger soft golden yellow blooms set off against light green foliage. In warmer climates it can be grown as a large shrub or as a small climber.

R. glauca or *R. rubifolia* is a species found in the mountains of central Europe. It is at its best draped over an old stone wall, where it can display its silver-purple foliage to advantage. Good in the shade, it truly is a rose that is grown mainly for its foliage as its flowers, pale lilac-pink, are insignificant, although they do lead to small vase-shaped purple hips in autumn. It will grow to 2.5 m and also makes a wonderful mounded shrub.

The Cassiorhodon roses are found through the northern United States and across Europe from the Balkans to Korea. *R. farreri persetosa*, the Threepenny-bit Rose, with its ferny leaves that colour well in the autumn, has tiny lavender-pink flowers and masses of small tomato-red hips. It is a very engaging shrub and does particularly well in shade, covering an area of 2 m. *R. fedtschenkoana* is one of those roses that grows into a massive and magnificent shrub. In the spring it produces masses of single white tissue-like flowers, which smother the bush and look wonderful against the pale sea-green foliage. The flowers are repeated but not in such mass. In autumn the plant produces bottle-shaped hips of bristly orange or tomato-red. With its branches of 3 m, it needs space and can be a great specimen plant.

The Rugosas mentioned for their hips in chapter 11 are good collectors' roses, but so are 'F. J. Grootendorst' and 'White Grootendorst' for the continuous display of their most unusual carnation-shaped flowers. An interesting hybrid that is continuously in flower and produces a strong perfume and lots of hips is 'Corylus'. The growth is very close and erect to approximately 1.2 m, and the flowers are single, a silvery lavender-pink with dull gold stamens. Unlike the tough foliage of most Rugosas, this is more feathery

R. multiflora hedge

and is a rich warm green that produces great colours in the autumn — an excellent hedge rose. 'Fimbriata' or 'Phoebe's Frilled Pink' is another good variety of this species. With small white and soft pink flowers in clusters, it is quite erect in growth to 1.5 m.

No collection should be without *R. arvensis*, the English Field Rose, as it is known, or the similar hybrid 'Dundee Rambler', which has a rather more dense habit of growth. *R. arvensis* has the small single white flowers with gold stamens typical of a rambler, and 'Dundee Rambler' is double. They are good for using for reflections in ponds or as woodland ramblers.

At Roseneath a rather ugly line of casuarinas (the Australian she-oak) has been topped to 4 m high and through this a mass planting of *R. multiflora*, that weed that is often used as a rootstock, with its small single white flowers in massive clusters, and *R. multiflora cathayensis*, the pink form, foams out, forming a truly magical hedge. *R. multiflora*, because of its use in the breeding of many roses, right up to modern hybrids, deserves a place in any serious collection.

A few Multiflora ramblers are also worth including. 'Rambling Rector' is one of the best roses for covering an eyesore or climbing into a tree, with its great masses of clusters of loosely double off-white flowers. Very shade-tolerant, it will grow to a height of over 8 m. 'Ghislaine de Féligonde' is best used as a pillar rose, with its double apricot-salmon flowers repeating well in warmer climates. 'Phyllis Bide' is another raggedy salmon double flower that repeats well and is good as a pillar rose.

'Russelliana', a Multiflora rambler with a sweet scent, has small double flowers that are a mixture of red and mauve, and is ideal used on a fence that

R. pendulina or *R. alpina*, the Alpine Rose

R. chinensis

127

you often walk past, enabling you to catch its strong perfume. Not as vigorous as many ramblers, it can be grown as a large shrub. It will succeed in a shady area but really performs in the warmth of the sun. Another Multiflora, 'Rose Marie Viaud', is a seedling of the lilac-purple rambler 'Veilchenblau' and is similar to it except for being slightly more double. It is excellent in trees to 6 m.

We owe a lot to *R. chinensis* and the China roses like 'Old Blush China' for many newer hybrids, and with their long flowering season they deserve a place in any collection. There are many forms of *R. chinensis*, and the variety we have at Roseneath is a single deep rosy reddish pink that grows to about 6 m. It is constantly in flower and often has the peculiarity of flowering at its best in winter. 'Old Blush China', or 'Parsons' Pink China' as it is often called after the man who introduced it to England in 1789, is also constantly in flower. A loose double of soft satin-pink with rosier tonings, it is virtually free of thorns and comes as both bush and climber. The bush form grows to 2 m and the climber to about 5 m or so, and both are tolerant of shade. Another China rose, *R. turkestanica*, or 'Mutabilis' as it is widely known, grows into a large shrub which smothers itself in single flowers that range in colour from soft salmon to rosy pink. It is constantly in flower. One of the most unusual of the Chinas is 'Viridiflora', the Green Rose. It has flowers with petals that have never properly formed; they are still set back in time like half-developed leaves. Constantly blooming on a 1 m shrub, this rose is a florist's dream as it is an ideal cut flower. Some people find it interesting whereas others think it's awful.

'Viridiflora'

OTHER ROSES FOR
THE COLLECTOR'S GARDEN

R. banksiae	'Bourbon Queen'
R. x *cantabrigiensis*	'Charles de Mills'
R. x *dupontii*	'Chloris'
R. filipes	'Conditorum'
R. x *harisonii*	'Indica Major'
R. laevigata	'La Belle Sultane'
R. moyesii	'Louis XIV'
R. roxburghii	'Mignonette'
R. sweginzowii	'Mrs John Laing'
'Achievement'	'Roseraie de l'Hay'
'Adam'	'Soleil d'Or'

PART III

COMPANIONS
&
COLOUR SCHEMES

CHAPTER 14

Ideas for colour schemes

Colour is one of the fundamental joys of gardening. Through it we have a unique chance to express ourselves creatively, to develop something of the artist within, to have the sort of fun and possibly achieve the sense of satisfaction many of us will not really have experienced since we last dabbled with paint at school. But herein lies something of a dilemma, for we are no longer children with no concept of our ability or otherwise. Far from it — we are only too painfully aware that gardening these days is considered once

Nancy Steen used grey-foliaged plants to enhance pink and purple roses

'Parade' on an arch above pink silene; the combination of deep and light
pinks is enhanced by the grey-leaved *Elaeagnus angustifolia*

again to be a form of fine art and therefore the possibility of failure looms
large.

There are basically two ways of looking at the subject of colour in the
garden. First there is the interior decorator approach in which you advance
from your perfectly co-ordinated dwelling into the garden and inflict upon
that space the discriminating eye of the *exterior* decorator — an entirely valid
approach because it is based on making your living environment an agree-
able, soothing, harmonious place in which to spend your time. The second
approach is to toss the colour wheel unceremoniously out the window and get
out there and dabble, unleash the child artist buried within, wallow in those
wonderful moments when everything comes together and try to turn your
back on the rest. Fundamental to success or failure, of course, will be your
knowledge and understanding of the plants themselves — your skill as a
gardener. With either approach you need to know what will grow where and
when it will be doing what, as well as what size and shape it may be expected
to attain. A collection of rare and exotic species may be totally absorbing to its
owner and interesting intellectually, but it is never going to appeal to the
senses in the way that a carefully crafted garden tapestry will remind us of the
illusive beauty of a painted canvas.

The best solution is really a mixture of the two basic approaches, in
which you try to create a living environment which is essentially restful (and

occasionally stimulating) to the soul while at the same time reserving certain places or times of the year for a bit of experimentation and indulgence in the sheer joy of colour. As you are dealing with living, three-dimensional plants, which have texture and shape, and may be exposed to strong sunlight or dense shade, you can't just take the colours of indoor paint and fabric outside without taking these factors into account; the colour scheme used inside the house may create a very different image outside. Another important consideration is the backdrop against which the garden is to sit. Do you have a soft green hedge, a brick, stone or concrete block wall, a painted wooden fence or rustic post or brush arrangement? If you are going to have masses of old roses, which ones will go with what?

The smaller the garden, the more skilful you are going to have to be with the use of colour, remembering that by using vertical surfaces and perhaps by adding even more in the form of pillars, pergolas, and arches, you will add to the size of the gardening space. The quality of light can vary from place to place, and a harsher light can make the pale pastel colours, suited to a softer light, look washed out or monotonous. There will also be distinct changes with the seasons, most notably with the green backdrop, which in turn will have an effect on the appearance of other colours in the garden. Also the colour of old roses will sometimes vary quite markedly, depending on whether they are growing in sun or shade, what the soil is like and how much water they receive. In the late summer flush of second flowers, colours are often much more pronounced and sometimes flowers are larger too; though there may be fewer of them, they tend to be that much more special.

So, what works? What do you really want to live with, especially where space is limited? You might like a clear bright colour like red, for example, in a painting on the wall but do you want the whole wall to be painted red? Do you want the garden to be full of red flowers most of the time? What can work surprisingly well is to group together plants of one colour. For example, placing different varieties of pink roses together in one area can make them become more interesting individually. The effect is to make the observer focus beyond colour to differences in shape, form and texture as these characteristics become predominant. A simple way of lifting a monochromatic scheme like this is to add a contrasting colour with a light, sensitive touch. With pinks, for example, a sweep of blue in the form of *Echium* 'Blue Bedder' can result in a beautiful garden scene, arrresting in its simplicity.

Before we go any further, we need to grapple with a bit of colour terminology so that we know exactly what we are talking about. The three primary colours are red, blue and yellow, and these may be mixed to produce all the other colours. A secondary colour is a mixture of two primaries; green, for example, is made by mixing yellow and blue. Complementary colours are those that lie opposite each other on the colour wheel, such as yellow and purple, or green and red; contrasting might be a better term to use here as people often say that colours complement each other perfectly when in fact

'Duchesse de Brabant' with *Echium* 'Blue Bedder'

A grouping of similar-coloured roses including 'White Sparrieshoop',
'Pink Grootendorst' and 'Yesterday'

they mean that they blend well or compliment each other. Harmonising colours are those that lie next to each other on the colour wheel as they share a pigment — red, orange and yellow, for example. The definition of harmony in a gardening sense is a combination or arrangement of plants to produce an artistically pleasing effect. Hue is just another name for colour; the value of a colour is how light or dark it is; and the intensity of a colour refers to its brightness or dullness — it will be most intense at its purest and increasingly dull as more grey is added.

As well as the basic colour terminology, you need to be aware of the effect plants of different colours will have on each other. Over time you will develop an almost instinctive feeling for these relationships, and the more you look at gardens and the arrangement of plants, the better you will get at discerning what works and what doesn't. Yellow will look much brighter, more orange, for example, if placed next to green, whereas it will look more green if placed next to red. The differences are enhanced as the colour seems to take on some of its next-door neighbour's complementary colour. So a pairing of true complementaries can be dazzlingly bright, as they show each other up or make each other stronger — think of bright red holly berries against their dark green leaves. If you wish, this effect can be toned down by adding grey or black in the form of duller tones or deeper, darker shades. It is interesting to note that if you mix complementary colours in equal amounts, you get grey.

A simple combination of greens and yellows using 'Graham Thomas' as the centrepiece supported by variegated foliage works well

Pairing complementary colours, like a yellow rose with purple *Aconitum napellus*, and 'Kirsten Poulsen' with rich green foliage, makes each one appear stronger

Our eyes are increasingly stimulated as colours approach a truly complementary relationship. They try to combine them as grey but as this is impossible, each colour appears brighter than it would next to a dull or neutral colour.

Light, as Newton demonstrated by shining it through a prism, is the combination of all colours. Black, on the other hand, is not a colour at all: it is the absence of light. White reflects all colours whereas black absorbs them. Yellow is the most luminous colour in the spectrum and can be used to lighten a potentially sombre colour like blue. White also can be wonderfully useful in separating clashing colours. It intensifies each colour, making it more true to itself, but if you place it between the offending objects, for example in the form of a group of foxgloves, the day may well be saved. White is a vital ingredient and should be used liberally to literally release the colour inherent in the garden. A simple white and green or gold and green scheme, for example, can be stunningly effective.

Sometimes nature gives us little hints, like the yellow at the centre of many flowers, perhaps in the form of prominent stamens. It has the effect of enhancing the colour of the flower, of bringing it to life. We can copy this on a larger planting scale to great effect.

Let's look for a minute at the descriptive terms used for certain colours. Pink, for example, may be described as apricot, salmon, copper, coral, rose, cerise, magenta, fuchsia, clear, blush, hot or shocking. Red may be blood, crimson, magenta, cerise, scarlet, cherry, rose, brick, maroon, wine, apple, fuchsia, tomato, raspberry, strawberry or plum. Or again yellow may be

Multi-coloured 'Mutabilis'   'English Garden' with poppies

buttercup, primrose, golden, buff, lemon, sulphur or canary — not easy
when you're wading through a catalogue looking for just the right shade of
pink, red, yellow or whatever. Generally speaking, it pays to go and look at
the real thing in a nursery or garden before you plunge, if this is feasible.

Gardening with colour to the fore need not be limiting. You can ring the
changes with the seasons to create quite different effects, just as Monet did at
Giverny, with the enormous curved archway of metal hoops leading to the
door of the big pink house, covered in spring with roses, peonies and
campanulas, then in summer all orangey red and yellow as the dahlias and
sunflowers take over and nasturtiums spread across the gravel path, almost
meeting in the middle.

Apart from Monet, Gertrude Jekyll and Vita Sackville-West have both
had an enormous influence on the way we think about colour in the garden
today. Through her books and the many gardens she designed, Gertrude
Jekyll showed others how colour could be used to create, in effect, artistic
visions or paintings which developed and changed and grew as time went by.
Something of a Renaissance woman, with her awesome knowledge and skill
in many different areas, she combined her understanding of colour with her
experience as a gardener to create, with painstaking care, living tapestries of
great beauty. In her garden at Sissinghurst and through her persuasive
writings, Vita Sackville-West furthered the cause by confirming the importance of colour used imaginatively and with artistic sensitivity. In New
Zealand, Nancy Steen, with her training as a professional artist, did much to
bring an awareness of colour to the gardening world. Her own borders were

carefully crafted to create the pleasing pictorial images in her mind. She advocated the use of grey-foliaged plants, for example, to set off the purple Gallica Roses 'to perfection'. If the flowers of any of her chosen foliage plants didn't fit into the colour scheme, she would nip off the buds before they opened. This sort of attention to detail and understanding of colour, texture and shape and the effects they have on each other guarantees success.

Green is the predominant background colour in most gardens, and some would say that there is so much variety in the range of greens and the effect different textures have on those shades that there is no need for flowers. While the ferny foliage of aquilegias or the soft green saucers of *Alchemilla mollis* are undeniably attractive and restful in the garden, I wouldn't want to be without the elusive beauty brought by the colour of flowers at some stage of the year. Let's not underestimate the effect that colour has on our emotions because this is an important aspect of our ultimate choices. A touch of yellow is bound to lighten and brighten; pink can be warm and red can be invigorating; blue can be dreamy and misty, or clear and fresh like the sea and sky on a summer's day, or chilling and depressing if it is not relieved with a little light in the form of a dash of white or touch of palest lemon. Violet and purple are powerful; traditional colours of the church, they command atten-

This pleasing combination includes 'Golden Showers' and 'Mutabilis' against the house and 'Anna Maria de Montravel' and 'Mme Lauriol de Barny' in front

tion. Green is soothing — the colour of life and hope. Interestingly, another property of colour is that 'warm' colours like red and yellow stand out or advance whereas 'cold' colours, like blue, fade or recede mistily into the distance.

Old roses come in a vast range of colours which are far removed from the often static, sharp bright hues of many of the modern Hybrid Teas and Floribundas. Many are soft subtle shades, in infinite varieties of pink and white and yellow, which change as they open from the bud, while the stronger pinks and cerise colours of the Rugosa family, with their cheerful hips, or the deep purple-reds of some of the Gallicas will add strength to any composition. Some of the tiny white-flowered ramblers in full flight up old trees look as if they were the blossom of the tree itself, cascading from great heights in swinging garlands. Others like the Albas or the Bourbons blend into mixed plantings without a ripple. This is the great beauty of the older varieties; they are shrubs and should be treated as such, melded into the rest of the garden, not isolated in special beds with bare earth at their feet. Nothing is more depressing than the sight of a bed of Hybrid Teas in the middle of winter. With clever underplanting, old roses need never look quite like that. If you have to prune them because of size, do so straight after they have flowered then you can let the perennials and other shrubs take over and fill the gap while the roses rest. Plants like salvias are excellent as they continue flowering into the winter. It never ceases to amaze me that people are perfectly happy to wait for their rhododendrons or their camellias, or at least to plant a range of varieties to ensure a longer display, whereas there is a great outcry about once-flowering roses. If you spread your planting among the different varieties and incorporate some of the new Austins and the odd acceptable hybrid, you won't have much time without colour in your garden. Quite simply, some things are worth waiting for.

Simple monochromatic schemes can be rewarding — like pale pink with deeper richer pinks, for example. If you want to play safe, the old favourite mix of pink and blue with a touch of white or palest yellow always looks good, but in the Southern Hemisphere, where the light is clear and bright, these colours may need to be strengthened to compensate. Using direct contrasts, which would look garish in the softer light of the English spring and early summer, is quite acceptable and often desirable. The milder climates of the Mediterranean, California, Australia, South Africa and New Zealand give rise to a more carefree, summery atmosphere, where people and gardens can wear brighter garments, and massed pastels are sometimes diluted by the glaring light to create a bleached, overexposed impression.

It is important to think of the whole plant, not just the full-blown flower when considering colour. If you prefer autumn tonings, the pink buds of 'Iceberg', for example, will irritate every time you see them, whereas the peachy ones of 'Avalanche' would have warmed and satisfied, yet both have white flowers. Be true to yourself and your garden will be rewarding.

Foliage is the vital backdrop and must never be underestimated or overlooked. Will the flowers of the rose provide accents with the leaves showing through the spaces or create a solid mass of colour? Are the leaves a light soft green, deep dark and leathery, glossy or matt, ferny or large, or are they heavily veined and robustly healthy as in the Rugosa family? Shape and size of flower in relation to the foliage and other garden shrubs and trees must be borne in mind. Multi-coloured light airy roses like 'Mutabilis' can create magical diffusing effects when used in front of dark forest-green shrubs or a woodland backdrop.

Hips and autumn foliage can provide fresh interest when the flowers are

Four roses with prominent stamens (clockwise from top left):
'Dainty Bess', 'Ellen Willmott', 'Golden Wings', 'White Wings'

Autumn foliage of *R. virginiana plena*

over, although sometimes flowers continue to appear on bushes bearing hips. A rose like *R. virginiana plena* provides strong autumn colour as its glossy leaves change with the season. The thorns of some roses are fascinating, none more so than the translucent ones of *R. sericea pteracantha*. Placed in front of a steely grey-green astelia or something light coloured to make them show up, they can be captivating.

The beauty of some roses lies in their prominent stamens: the single flowers of *R. laevigata*, 'Ellen Willmott', 'Dainty Bess', 'White Wings', 'Golden Wings' and 'Mermaid', and the nearly single 'Meg', all rely on pronounced stamens for their appeal. Others, like 'Erfurt', have contrasting centres as well as stamens for effect. 'Roger Lambelin' has curious white edges and markings on its dark wine-red petals, and striped roses like 'Rosa Mundi', 'Ferdinand Pichard' and 'Variegata di Bologna' are equally intriguing.

Colour is an element of fashion and style, and while that shouldn't dictate, it is part of the fun and forward-looking aspect of gardening. Flowers with a green tinge are currently sought after, and bolder orange-purple combinations which the last generation would have turned from in horror can be amazingly effective in the right hands. If these colours are too strong for your taste, soften them to apricot with blue-purples, and use companion plants in these colours, like deep blue-purple salvias, campanulas or irises with apricot roses. Yellow and blue is another winning combination, the yellow illuminating or enhancing the blue. Van Gogh recognised that without yellow and orange, blue virtually ceased to exist, so if you want your blue garden to come to life, add yellow or orange.

In a small city garden where brick predominates in walls and paths, you could choose a few roses that would suit this mellow old apricot-pink, red-brick background. The Hybrid Musks are particularly valuable here, because of their inherent subtlety, beginning with 'Penelope' or perhaps the deeper 'Felicia', both of which will grow well against a wall. The New English Rose 'Abraham Darby' is equally suitable, and perhaps the more apricot 'Jaquenetta', depending on the toning of the bricks. 'Ghislaine de Féligonde' is another old rambler of wonderfully subtle colouring. 'Albertine' is useful here because it is a salmon coppery pink, not a clear blue-pink. 'Lady Waterlow' has a hint of yellow and peach about it beneath the pink veining.

Against a green background, hedge or tree or with a strong lawn base, I would use white, perhaps with lemon tonings like 'Albéric Barbier', for example, or 'Wedding Day', the White Banksia, *R. lævigata* or *R.* x *dupontii* (which looks wonderful in a tree). The Noisette 'Lamarque' would be ideal, with its creamy yellow tints. The small-flowered rambler 'Sanders' White' makes a good standard to give height in a small garden, with its exquisite flowers cascading downwards. 'Sea Foam' is equally useful where this kind of treatment is desirable. Alternatively, it can be used as ground-cover cascading down banks.

You could bring some light and warmth to a cold grey stone wall with yellows or alternatively pinks, but they would have to be blue-pinks like 'Fantin-Latour', 'Lavender Lassie', 'Constance Spry' or 'Mary Rose', without a hint of orange in them. 'Mermaid' is a magnificent single yellow rambler which can reach enormous proportions. 'Leverkusen' is semi-double, with interestingly ragged petals. A very luminous rose, useful for

'Joseph's Coat' and 'Moonlight' (below)   'Ghislaine de Féligonde'

lightening, it would be good in a slightly shady place. Its pale lemon colour provides a wonderful contrast with a rich velvety red or the deep violet-blue of aconitums.

'Lawrence Johnston' is a vigorous superbly fragrant yellow climber with light green foliage, named by Graham Thomas after the creator of Hidcote, who rescued it from obscurity when he bought it from Pernet-Ducher in France. They had originally rejected it in favour of its sister seedling 'Le Rêve', which is a little softer and less vigorous. 'Easlea's Golden Rambler' is another desirable yellow climber with dark glowing foliage, wonderful flowing over a large tankstand or old shed.

Against rustic fences, trellis or bare wood, yellow climbers like 'Céline Forestier' and 'Crépuscule' would be useful, the latter inclining towards apricot. 'Meg' is decidedly apricot and stunning, with its large single flowers in clusters. Equally striking is the very double 'Alchemist', with a richer peachy yellow centre. The older 'Gloire de Dijon' is a similar buff-yellow with a more reliably quartered shape, like its parent, 'Souvenir de la Malmaison'. 'Desprez à Fleurs Jaunes' and 'Phyllis Bide' are almost mixtures of yellow and pink, perfect in the right place, perhaps with a glossy dark green background. 'Windrush' is a gentle pale yellow semi-double bush which grows large in warm climates, as does 'Golden Wings', which is a little deeper and is a lovely single rose that can easily be kept small if necessary.

A grouping of reds using 'Parade' and 'The Bishop' with
contrasts of blue and white aquilegias

142

'Green Ice' — flowers with a green tinge are popular

R. hugonis, the Golden Rose of China, has lovely primrose-yellow flowers and ferny foliage, while 'Graham Thomas' is the ultimate yellow statement, rich and strong, perfect for southern climes or anywhere.

White climbers and ramblers with pink buds or tints include 'Mme Alfred Carrière', or the exquisite 'Adélaide d'Orléans', moving through to the deeper 'Paul Transon' and 'François Juranville'. 'New Dawn' is pale pink, useful in light shade; 'Constance Spry' likewise. 'Sparrieshoop' is a clear pink with lighter centres, single in large clusters, a good rose to grow below a high verandah or deck where you can look down into the upright faces of the flowers. 'Tausendschön' can be grown as a large shrub or used to ramble over archways. The lower-growing 'Duchesse de Brabant' is hard to beat as a clear pink, as is 'Ballerina', with its big clusters of tiny pink and white flowers. 'Dapple Dawn' is a large single pink with a paler or even white centre, suitable for the back of the border or against a wall. 'Complicata' is similar but a slightly deeper pink, while 'Clair Matin' is another lovely pale pink single. Other David Austins are 'Mary Rose' and 'The Reeve', both good clear blue-pinks. 'Belle Amour' has alluring rounded blooms in a perfect shade of salmon-pink. The Rugosa 'Frau Dagmar Hastrup' has clear pink single flowers of great appeal. A modern climber of a stronger pink is 'Pink Perpétue', a perfectly formed rose with beautifully sculpted buds.

I have a friend who dislikes any roses tending toward the lilac, mauve or purple shades, saying they depress her as they remind her of old ladies and Victoriana! It's eternally fascinating how different people can be. I think I like them for that very reason — they bring out that sense of nostalgia and, to my mind, something of the past preserved for the future. Look at how

143

'Veilchenblau'

lavender has become the plant of the moment, just another example of our desire to capture something of the past which, after all, works exceedingly well as a garden plant. And where would we be without violets? That said, I would not want lilac and purple everywhere all the time but enjoy it in the Gallicas and purple-flowered ramblers such as 'Veilchenblau' when they appear. These colours stand out well against white or pale cream painted walls and fences and are enhanced by flowers of these lighter shades. Again, it is a matter of what you put next to them that often determines the effect they will have on your psyche. 'Cardinal de Richelieu', 'Hippolyte' and 'Anaïs Ségales' are other Gallicas in purple-red tones. 'Ripples' and 'Katherine Mansfield' are modern roses in paler mauve.

What about those rich warm reds? In a larger garden you can use plenty of them, but in a restricted space some measure of belt-tightening is wise. Another point is the way they get burnt quickly in intense sunshine, so careful placement is necessary. A little shade from a deciduous cherry tree or similar plant can work well. 'Parade' is a good cerise or rosy pink-red, while 'Sophie's Perpetual' is similar but with the addition of white undertones. 'Étoile de Hollande' is a true blood-red, as is the more recent 'Dublin Bay', a McGredy rose bred from the successful 'Bantry Bay' and 'Altissimo'. 'Wilhelm' is a Hybrid Musk in crimson-red tones, while 'Scharlachglut' is a lower-growing scarlet single Gallica hybrid bred by Kordes. White in the form of daisies, perhaps, or gypsophila can be superb with red, and a light clear yellow with a true blood-red can also be a dramatic combination.

144

'Cardinal de Richelieu'

Many of the Rugosas incline towards strong magentas or fuchsia-pinks so they need to be sensitively placed too. Grey is usually an excellent foil for these blue-toned reds, or even the blue of water in the background to give a cooling effect. Their own healthy crinkled foliage lends them added weight as strong shrubs in the garden, and most of them have generous red hips as well.

Awareness of colour is the key to success in using it in the garden. By carefully observing how it is used and the effect it has on us in other people's gardens as well as our own, we can begin to develop ideas for successfully combining different hues to create a pleasing result. Gardens are exceedingly personal, and ultimately it will come down to personal preference, but what an intensely satisfying experience when we get it right, even if it's only one of those tiny incidents that more often than not occur by chance!

CHAPTER 15

Companion planting

The success or otherwise of a garden based on old roses lies partly in the skill of the gardener in planting appropriate companions for those old roses. After all, one of their greatest attractions lies in the fact that they neither need nor wish to sit in isolated splendour. With whom, then, do they prefer to mingle? First of all the association must be aesthetically pleasing, the colours must harmonise with, or enhance, those of the roses, and they should provide further interest later in the summer and into the autumn when some of the roses will not be in flower.

In its time, the rose has been valued for many things, not least its importance as a herb. Many people come to old roses via herbs and some the other way round, and this is probably a good place to look for plants that seem 'at home' with old-fashioned roses. Some of the most useful are to be found in

'Old Blush China' with purple *Salvia horminum*

The white Hybrid Musk 'Prosperity', pink lavateras and blue-purple delphiniums, highlighted by the yellow *Thalictrum flavum speciosum* behind

the sage or *Salvia* family, many of which are reliable and attractive, with long flowering periods. Clary sage, *S. sclarea* var. *turkestanica*, has silvery pink bracts, and the annual *S. horminum* is pink and white with darker pink bracts. 'Black Knight' is a stunning variety of *S. guarantica*, with inky blue flowers all summer and autumn. Canary Island sage, *S. canariensis*, has purple-rose-coloured flowers and interesting foliage. Two other salvias to consider are *S. leucantha*, with woolly violet-purple flowers, and *S. mexicana*, with green bracts followed by deep blue flowers. The best blue of all, to my mind, is the tall *S. azurea*, although swathes of the brighter *S. uliginosa* planted en masse look superbly willowy in late summer.

Lavender, in all its many varieties, seems a natural companion for old roses. The grey-green foliage works well with the pinks through to the deep dark purples of the rose blooms, and the lilacs, pinks and whites of the lavender flowers blend easily. Lavender hedges can be used to replace the traditional box, but choose the right kind for your purpose. In warmer climates *Lavandula dentata* grows almost too well and is inclined to become ungainly, as it flowers all year round and there is no obvious trimming time. *L. stoechas*, French lavender, is useful for hedging, and so are some of the English varieties like 'Munstead' and 'Hidcote Purple' or the pink *L. rosea*. Many of these are now available in dwarf sizes.

All the catmints or catnips suit old roses too, being similar to the lavenders, with their grey-green foliage and soft violet-blue flowers. *Nepeta* x *faassenii* is probably the most useful as a border, or you can use the larger-growing 'Six Hills Giant' within the bed itself.

Dianthus or pinks offer the same grey foliage and make a superb border to any beds which have low walls edging them. Many have desirable fragrance, and there are plenty of suitable colours to choose from in this family. Common garden pinks or the smaller tufted perennial forms are largely derived from *D. plumarius* and they include old favourites like the fringed white clove-scented 'Mrs Sinkins'. Laced pinks have particular charm, with their dark centres and borders, while many forms just have a dark centre. Sweet William or *D. barbatus*, with its larger flatter heads made up of many tiny flowers, can be particularly good with some of the stronger red roses in a more dynamic colour scheme.

The yarrow family is virtually essential in one form or another. *Achillea ptarmica* 'The Pearl' is a superb ground-cover, its little white button flowers bringing much cheer in late summer. *A. millefolium* or common yarrow has little white flowers, or there is the pink *A. roseum*. Many of the salmon and creamy yellow cultivars now on offer fit well with certain roses, like 'Muta-bilis', for example.

Flowering chives or onions, alliums, are always attractive, their spiky

'Archiduc Joseph' and tall mignonette, *Reseda alba*, with *Lavandula dentata* in the foreground shows how cottage garden plants provide a perfect foil for old roses

Achillea 'Apple Blossom' provides a continuing display after the
flowers of 'Desprez à Fleurs Jaunes' have finished

round mauve heads providing a relief from the focused faces of open single
flower forms.

The many varieties of wallflower are invaluable, flowering on and on as
they do, in all their various colours. *Cheiranthus mutabilis* changes through
mauve, purple and apricot. 'Bowles Mauve' is often thought to be a wallflower but is really an *Erysimum* which has the same incredibly long flowering
habit — ten months of the year. The spikes bear deep purple buds which
open to reveal lavender-lilac flowers, each one lasting for weeks with replace-
ments constantly at hand.

The following herbs deserve consideration too. The blue-flowering form
of hyssop, *Hyssopus officinalis*, can be used like lavender or catmint, as a
hedge or just a bushy upright ground-cover. Rosemary, with its lavender-blue
flowers, can be used in the same way, being especially useful for dry corners.
Valerian officinalis, or true valerian, has white or pale pink fragrant flowers.
Centranthus ruber 'Alba' is the ordinary white valerian. Rue, *Ruta graveolens*
'Jackman's Blue' has fine but rounded glaucous foliage and yellow flowers in
summer. *Thalictrum* or meadow rue has lovely ferny foliage, especially *T.
dipterocarpum*, with its delicate sprays of lilac flowers opening from little balls
to reveal yellow stamens. *T. flavum glaucum* (*T. f. speciosum*) has yellow flowers.
Hesperis matronalis, or sweet rocket, fits in perfectly with a cottage-garden
style, and its lilac flowers are scented at night. Sweet cicely, *Myrrhis odorata*,
has sweet-smelling fern-like leaves with flat heads of little white flowers.
Bergamot, *Monarda didyma*, comes in some soft pink shades such as 'Croft-
way Pink' or 'Prairie Glow', or the deep reddish purple 'Prairie Night',
although other reds can be too strong for some old roses. A really valuable
filler for flowering on into autumn is that old standby feverfew. The decorative

The lime-green *Euphorbia epithymoides* highlights the yellow
centre of 'Fritz Nobis'

double form of this little white *Chrysanthemum parthenium* is my favourite.

The white daisy flowers of *Boltonia asteroides* are also good value in the autumn. The Australian daisies *Brachyscome multifida* and the cultivar 'Break o' Day' have mauve and deeper lavender flowers respectively all year long above fine lacy leaves.

Alchemilla mollis has to be one of the best foils for old roses, with its large rounded grey-green leaves and funny tufts of fluffy lime flowers, adding those desirable ingredients texture and form by the bucketful to any garden. The euphorbias provide the same service and are invaluable for filling in dry shady areas. Sedums are the answer in hot dry places.

Aquilegias, granny's bonnets or columbines, are ideal as underplanting for old roses, especially the older pure-coloured varieties like the blue *Aquilegia* 'Hensoll Harebell' or some of the pinks, which range from softest blush to deep dusky pinks, or white. Their foliage is some of the loveliest in the garden, remaining coolly green and fern-like throughout the summer, and they have the added advantage of self-seeding happily and lending an established 'been here for ever' air to the garden. If you want to keep coloured varieties 'true', separate them well as they will cross with others readily.

Verbenas come in a wide range of colours and are outstanding carpeting plants for that sunny spot at the front of the border as they spread readily and flower freely. Some of them are available in wonderfully subtle shades, like the blended apricot-peach and cream of 'Peaches and Cream'. *Lamium* or deadnettle is another invaluable ground-covering plant for partial shade. 'White Nancy' has pure white flowers and silvery striped leaves, and pale pink and stronger mauve-pink forms are also available.

There are plenty of useful yellows to choose from. *Potentilla recta* 'Warrenii' has soft yellow single flowers. *Sisyrinchium striatum* throws up starry creamy yellow flowers on tall spires, making it a superb accent plant. The evening primrose (*Oenothera*) comes in pinks, lemons and whites — low-growing like *O. speciosa*, which has soft pink flowers and spreads as a ground-cover; medium-sized and bushy like *O. pallida*, which has large fragrant white flowers; or tall like the biennial *O. biennis*, which has clear yellow flowers. The lovely annual pale creamy yellow *Eschscholzia caespitosa* or California poppy is ideal for adding a touch of luminescence.

The true geraniums or cranesbills are perfect for massing with old roses, having plenty of foliage and a good range of pink, blue and white flowers borne over a long period. Some of the best are: *G. endressii* 'Wargrave Pink', silvery salmon-pink with pale green foliage; *G.* 'Claridge Druce', taller with mauve-pink flowers and grey-green foliage; *G. pratense*, deep violet-blue; *G. pratense* 'Albuma'; *G. himalayense*, large blue veined flowers and finely cut leaves; *G. wallichianum* 'Buxton's Blue', blue flowers with an attractive white centre and light green leaves; *G.* 'Johnson's Blue', irresistible violet-blue flowers and daintily cut leaves; and *G. sanguineum album*.

'Sea Foam' with *Brachyscome multifida* 'Break o' Day'

151

Diascia rigescens is invaluable where salmon-pink is required and will trail happily over walls. *Diascia* 'Ruby Fields' has deeper pink flowers from late spring right through autumn.

Many of the penstemons are ideal companions, with their long flowering period and superb colours. 'Garnet' is a deep red, 'Susan' and 'Apple Blossom' are soft pinks, and 'Purple Passion' has deep purple flowers. There are blues, too, like the subtly blended 'Stapleford Gem' or clear 'True Blue'.

The annual lavateras or mallows produce a tremendous show when the roses are often resting, *Lavatera trimestris* 'Mont Blanc', 'Loveliness' and 'Silver Cup' are white, soft pink and bright pink respectively. The perennial mallows like *L. thuringiaca* 'Barnsley' are ideal in a large garden but can always be trimmed to fit their allotted space in a smaller area. *Sidalcea malviflora* 'Starks Hybrids' have similarly striking flowers on tall spires.

Cerinthe major or honeywort, with its red and yellow flowers, and *C. major* 'Purpurescens', the purple form, add a hint of the wild garden, as does *Orlaya grandiflora*, a form of white parsley rather like Queen Anne's lace. An alternative to true Queen Anne's lace, *Daucus carota*, providing the same filling effect as gypsophila, is the bishop's flower, *Ammi majus*. There is also an attractive fern-leaf variety, *Ammi visnaga*. The toadflaxes or linarias are equally invaluable for adding this touch of gay abandonment. Like miniature antirrhinums, they grow much taller and their light feathery appearance

Cerinthe major 'Purpurescens', nigella and poppies create a rich
tapestry effect with old roses

'Felicia' with nicotianas and geraniums

makes them ideal wherever you need to bring some height into a casual, cottagey garden. The pink is called *Linaria purpurea* 'Canon Went', while the purple form is just *L. purpurea*. The perennial nemesias have similar flowers but are lower growing.

Silenes, commonly known as campions or catchflies, are linked to the *Lychnis* family and add to the wild flower image with their pink or white flowers, as do the simple corn cockles and soapworts, like the rather straggly *Saponaria officinalis* or 'Bouncing Bet'.

The finer old-fashioned forms of viola like heartsease are ideal for carpeting the ground beneath roses, so long as they don't have the larger pansy-like heads which would vie for attention. *Viola tricolor* 'Miss Helen Mount' is the charming old-fashioned three-coloured viola with white, purple and yellow markings; *V. tricolor* 'King Henry' is deep purple with a yellow centre; *V. cornuta*, the horned violet, has lovely white forms called *V. cornuta alba* and 'White Perfection', as well as a cream version known as 'Cream Princess'. Two forms of *V. wittrockiana* well worth growing for their long flowering period and attractive little round faces are 'Baby Lucia', a deep blue with yellow eye, and 'Baby Franjo', a cheerful yellow. Other possibilities in the violet family are the sweet-scented old-fashioned varieties recreated in New Zealand by Kerry Carman. Many of the older forms so loved by the Victorians were brought out to the Antipodes by early settlers and were carefully preserved by subsequent generations. Kerry has collected many of these from around the country and brought them together so that nature could again produce some of the old favourites. They range in colour from

An Alba diffused by the effect of a random planting of
foxgloves (*Digitalis*)

deep purple, lilac and white through the whole range of pinks, with the same evergreen mat-forming foliage of more modern varieties.

Nicotianas — white, green, pink, red, or the delightful green bell-shaped flowers on long stems of *Nicotiana langsdorfii* — all fit well with an old-fashioned theme. *N. sylvestris* has sprays of long white flowers with that superb nicotiana scent of balmy summer evenings.

Swainsona galegifolia 'Alba' is a charming perennial with little white pea-shaped flowers. Another graceful addition to an older style of rose garden is *Dierama pulcherrimum*, commonly known as lady's wand.

If you envisage swathes of blue, you might consider the following plants. *Nigella* or love-in-the-mist, *Nemophila* or the California bluebell, *Nolana*, cornflowers and larkspurs are all useful annuals, their blues, pinks and whites blending in well with the roses. Forget-me-nots, too, are always right, in whatever shade. *Omphalodes cappadocica* is a delightful perennial with clear blue flowers just like forget-me-nots but a little deeper. It grows well in shade so is ideal for underplanting. For open sunny spots, use the low-growing *Echium* 'Blue Bedder', perfect with true pink roses with no hint of apricot. The perennial form of the cornflower, *Centaurea montana*, comes in striking blue, deep pink or white varieties, which look like the annual form but are larger and more open. The perennial *Lobelia syphilitica*, quite unlike the common annual lobelia spilling out of tubs and hanging baskets, is worth adding. A charming perennial form which looks the same and has the same growth habit as the annual form is called 'Minstrel' and is a light Cambridge blue with a lavender tinge. Another useful blue is Jacob's ladder, *Polemonium caeruleum*. *Scabiosa* or the pin-cushion flower has lovely flattish heads of lavender-blue. The willowy *Viscaria* 'Blue Angel' is always a highlight massed in a mixed border. A final blue choice would be *Convolvulus mauritanicus*, an excellent trailing plant to spill over walls. Its delightful single lilac-blue flowers are borne prolifically, especially in sunnier spots.

Campanulas or bell flowers are made for blending with old roses, either the taller-growing *Campanula persicifolia*, *C. glomerata lactiflora* or *latifolia* or the carpeting *C. poscharskyana* or *carpatica*. Platycodons or balloon flowers belong to the same family and come in some equally beautiful shades of blue. It is fascinating the way they open from attractive tightly closed 'balloons' into almost star-shaped bells.

For height, you can use foxgloves or *Digitalis*, *Aconitum* or monkshood, lilies, the tall mignonette, *Gaura lindheimeri*, *Cosmos* or *Cleome*, opium poppies, hollyhocks, delphiniums, watsonias, irises or those wonderful spiring verbascums. For a slice of real drama insert some towering *Echium fastuosum*, entirely in keeping with an old-fashioned theme.

Many of the herbs already mentioned provide silver-grey foliage, which is excellent in the form of small hedges or edging to frame the beds or borders. Other plants to give this silvery grey effect include the well-known *Stachys* or lamb's ear, *S. olympica* 'Silver Carpet' being the best for this purpose, and *Lychnis*, preferably *L. coronaria* 'Alba'. The artemisias have more finely cut silver and grey foliage and there are many different varieties to choose from, some of the best being *A. absinthium* 'Lambrook Silver', *A.* 'Powis Castle', *A. ludoviciana* 'Silver King' and *A. arborescens*. Another useful ground-cover

R. sericea pteracantha offset by *Astelia chathamica*, and 'Safrano' in front of *Phormium* 'Bronze Baby'

Lavender hebe with 'Bantry Bay'

plant with very similar fine silvery grey foliage is *Eriocephalus africanum*. The New Zealand native *Astelia chathamica* is a stunning perennial, with its long sword-like silvery leaves lending grace and form to any part of the garden. *Lysimachia ephemerum* has long pointed grey-green leaves and tall spikes of tiny white flowers, adding a useful height dimension.

Turning from annuals and perennials to shrubs, *Philadelphus* work in well, as do deutzias, their soft flowers never threatening to dominate the roses. *Spiraea* 'Anthony Waterer' goes well with some of the cerise-pink roses, being somewhat similar to the pinky red forms of *Achillea*. The hibiscus lookalike *Alyogyne huegelii* has lilac flowers which look superb with apricot-salmon roses.

The Californian poppy, *Romneya coulteri*, has fine grey-green foliage and then enormous papery white flowers. It is useful for associating with once-flowering roses as it will flower when they have finished. *Cistus* have charming single flowers in white and cerise-pink and can also be useful in hot, dry parts of the garden. *Convolvulus cneorum* contributes its silvery foliage as well as its appealing single white flowers to the rose garden.

Other plants I always think associate well and are useful for shadier areas are the abutilons, so long as they are kept in check and perhaps with the exception of the orange variety, depending of course on the particular roses you are associating them with. *Abutilon vitifolium* from Chile has soft grey-green leaves and the loveliest mallow-type flowers of lilac-blue, or there is a white variety, 'Album'.

'Mrs R. M. Finch' with *Achillea* 'Cerise Queen'

Old roses frame a pathway meandering through this old-fashioned garden

Nancy Steen loved to grow fuchsias with old roses, believing that it was a practical combination as the fuchsias provide colour when the old roses are not in flower. Her training and skill as an artist further enabled her to arrange them to advantage, because, as she wrote, 'their colours harmonise perfectly'.

The hybrid clematis are an excellent choice with climbing roses as they are not too rampant and can be cut right back every year. They are perfect companions for old roses grown on chains between posts, the *viticella* and *jackmanii* hybrids in their many varieties being the best forms for this purpose; the others are too rampant and would swamp the roses.

The graceful hebes come in perfect colours for harmonising with old roses, and their contrasting form is a failproof method of adding interest. Apart from these attributes, they are among the easiest of plants to grow, thriving whatever you do to them. 'Inspiration' is an excellent purple form; 'Lilac Gem' and 'Lavender Lace' are reliable paler mauves. Outstanding white forms include *H. townsonii* 'Snowdrift', and *H. divaricata*; while *H.* 'Wiri Joy' is a good pink variety. The little parahebes are particularly appealing in white or lilac and are excellent over low walls.

Hoherias are useful backdrop trees, flowering in autumn when other interest is on the wane. Some of the many varieties of *Pittosporum* provide a fine-leaved background of softest green. Grey-leaved trees include the eucalyptus, olive or silver pear, the latter almost a garden cliché now, unfortunately, not that overuse can detract from its inherent charm. Old fruit trees make ideal props for climbing roses, or you can use almost any deciduous tree; it is hard for the roses to get enough sun when a dense evergreen is used for support, although they will try to find their way out to the light.

White or cream-coloured roses are seen to advantage against the dark red and purple-leaved varieties of certain trees and shrubs, like *Prunus cerasifera* 'Pissardii', *Cotinus* or smoke tree and *Berberis*. Bear in mind, however, the need for restful green areas and the different effects which evolve as the seasons change. Even in a tiny garden, there is usually a shady side or corner which can be turned into an oasis full of cool green plants like hostas, bergenias, camellias or ferns to counterbalance the roses and flowering perennials which predominate elsewhere.

PART IV

A YEAR IN THE OLD ROSE GARDEN

CHAPTER 16

A seasonal guide to planting, pruning, spraying and general care

Roses are very hardy plants which survive most conditions, but they need constant year-round care to perform and live up to their reputation of being the queen of garden plants. They will grow anywhere except in wet, boggy ground, where they will just wither and die. They can be left to their own defences, but if they are, they will tend to become overgrown and unruly, full of branches that will no longer flower. Diseases such as black spot, rust, and powdery and downy mildew will appear, and without liberal amounts of manure and water, plants will become shy and not flower readily. From the time they are planted until the day they display their first spring blooms, and on through spring and autumn until they become almost dormant, roses need to be pampered and cared for to get the best results.

LATE AUTUMN–WINTER: PLANTING

Roses used to be available in winter only, bare-rooted, but these days, like all garden shrubs, container-grown roses are available all year round. However, late autumn to mid-winter is really the best time to plant, and this is also when bare-rooted plants are readily available.

Most roses these days are budded onto a virus-free stock; for example, a rose like 'Queen Elizabeth' is budded or grafted onto a cutting-grown plant of a specially selected form of *R. multiflora*. This very strong and easy-to-grow rambler with a good root system gives the bud of 'Queen Elizabeth' a vigorous start, enabling it to grow to a good-sized specimen in one or two years.

160

Choose the strongest-looking plant available. If it's bare-rooted, check that the roots are sturdy and reasonably well trimmed. There should be two or three solid branches emerging from the stem at the union, where the bud has been grafted onto the stock. Although the roots on a container-grown rose are not visible, vigorous growth indicates good health.

A budded plant may send out a shoot from the stock below the bud union. This will generally be more vigorous in growth than the rest of the plant and will have smaller, narrower and different-coloured leaves. It must be removed, and there are two ways to go about this: one is by very firmly pushing it down and away from the stem, which will take out the growing eye; the second method, particularly if the growth is coming from below the ground, is to uncover it and, with a sharp knife, cut the growing shoot out.

Where possible, it is best to prepare the site a month or so before planting. Dig some organic compost into the topsoil and fork some of this into the subsoil with lime and rose or general garden fertiliser. At planting time, dig a hole larger than the spread of the roots, down to the subsoil, and fork in a handful of long-term, slow-release fertiliser. If the rose is to be planted near an established tree, a large hole, approximately half a cubic metre, should be dug about 1 m from the tree and filled with good soil and compost. Make a mound in the hole and place the rose on top of this, spreading the roots out and down, covering them with more topsoil and consolidating the soil by lightly treading it down. Keep the bud union a bit above the soil level if you intend to mulch, and do not use too much fertiliser at planting time as you may burn the roots. Container-grown roses planted in late autumn, winter or early spring should be bare-rooted — that is, most of the potting mix should be shaken off and the roots spread out into the soil. This is because potting mix is generally lighter than soil and can act as a sponge, holding water around the roots, which roses dislike. Sites that are boggy should be drained, or raised beds should be created so the plants sit above the wet ground.

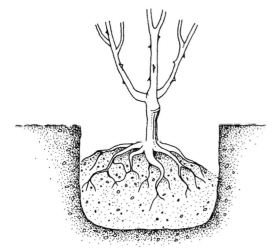

Correct planting: the roots are spread over a mound of soil

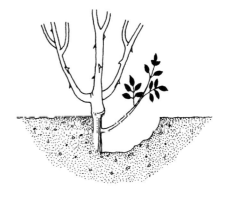

Suckers growing below the bud union should be removed

161

When you are planting roses as a hedge, the best guide is to plant the rose at an interval that is half the spread of its usual growth. If the rose is 2 m high, and 1.5 m wide, you would plant it 75 cm away from the next hedge plant. This is just a general guide; if you require a thicker and tighter hedge, you would need to plant the roses closer together.

Late autumn is also a good time to move any roses that have been planted in the wrong place. Perhaps you are changing a colour scheme, or the roses are too tall or too small for the location; whatever the reason, do it now. Prune the plant back hard then dig it out. Trim away any frayed or broken roots and replant, treating it as if it were a new plant. Quite large plants and climbers can be moved satisfactorily with care, and they will provide an instant garden in a new area.

This is also the time when gardens should be tidied and all old leaves raked up and taken away to be burned. Plants can now be given a good spraying of lime sulphur at winter strength to kill scale, fungous diseases and their spores; this also helps to defoliate the plants, readying them for pruning two to four weeks later.

LATE WINTER: PRUNING, PROPAGATING

Pruning is best done in late winter as early pruning can force growth too early and this can be easily damaged by a late cold snap. It's important always to use good tools and to keep them clean, sharp and well oiled. You will require a pair of secateurs, loppers for the heavier branches and a pruning saw. As you prune, take with you a jar full of strong disinfectant, like Jeyes fluid, in which to dip your tools or with which to wipe them as you go from plant to plant. This will help to stop the spread of diseases and viruses, which can be present in the sap and plant residues that are left on the tools.

Pruning old-fashioned roses is a very simple task but a very important one, for this is when you are adding shape to the plants and the garden, whether it be a cottage-style or rambling country garden. It can be done very quickly, basically paying attention to the shape and size of the plant.

All the bare-rooted roses that were planted earlier in the winter must now be repruned to outside eyes — in the nursery fields they have been very quickly and roughly pruned. This must also be done to newly planted container-grown roses as these have usually been left to grow untouched and need to be tidied up. Prune these back to about three buds high and again carefully select an outward-pointing eye, cutting slightly above it. This will enhance the shape of the bush, as the new shoots will grow away from the centre of the plant, giving a more open shape. It will also allow the sun to penetrate into the centre of the plant.

The older wood on once-flowering plants should have been trimmed hard back after flowering in late spring-early summer to force new growth for next season's flowering. The Gallicas, Albas, Centifolias and most Damasks should have been pruned in this way along with most ramblers and once-flowering climbers, but not plants that will have a crop of hips. In winter these roses should be pruned again, back one-third to outward-pointing buds, with the cut 5 mm above the bud and sloping away from it. Old and weak wood should be trimmed from the centre of the plant. Some of the shrub roses, particularly the Teas, can be pruned much harder, but it's important to try to balance the size of the bush with the size of the flower. For example, the large peachy pink flowers of 'Jean Ducher' look better on a big plant than on a small heavily pruned specimen. In a mixed border plants do not need to be symmetrically pruned; they can be shaped to fit in with the other plants around them. Species and their immediate hybrids, for example *R. moyesii*, *R. cantabrigiensis*, *R. sericea pteracantha* and 'Canary Bird', are best tidied up and not pruned back, except that old or weak wood should be removed to open up the centre of the plant.

Visitors to Roseneath often remark on the way we peg rose branches down. Where we have space, a 1–2 m branch is curved over and pegged to the ground. The flow of sap to all the buds along the branch is then more even, which enables the plant to produce up to ten times the number of flowers that it would produce if the branches were left to grow straight upwards.

The art of training and pruning climbers is to remember that the more horizontal the leaders are, the better they will flower. Keep the strong new basal shoots and tie them into the shape you wish to make and the area you wish to cover. Prune new climbing shoots back to pencil thickness or cut back up to one third, and shorten the old flower-stems that held last season's flowers to two or three buds from the main stem. This way as much of the strong new growth as possible is retained and two- or three-year-old wood as well as any weak or twiggy growth is removed. If you are planting on a fan-shaped wall trellis, you should keep as many new leaders as possible, about 60 cm apart, sloping outwards from the centre and as horizontal as possible.

If you are growing a rose on a pillar, it is best to keep three or four leaders and to bend them around the post as many times as you can to enable the maximum number of flowers to be produced. To prune a pillar rose, cut out the old wood and tidy the plant to the desired shape. If it is a thick-stemmed rose and you are unable to wind it around the pillar, cut the old wood back to approximately 60 cm from the ground and the younger two-year-old branches to 1.2 1.8 m, then prune the newest growth to 1.8–2 m. This will give a layered effect and a more even flower cover.

If you have planted a hedge of roses, it is best to prune them back hard in their first two years to create a thick, dense hedge. In the first year, cut the hedge back to at least 60 cm and in the second year to at least 90 cm. Once it is established, it can be pruned by clipping with hedge shears or by shortening the new growth and removing some of the oldest wood. Where ramblers are growing in existing hedges or on wires, the new growth can be left unpruned to flower the following year, giving an informal and loosely

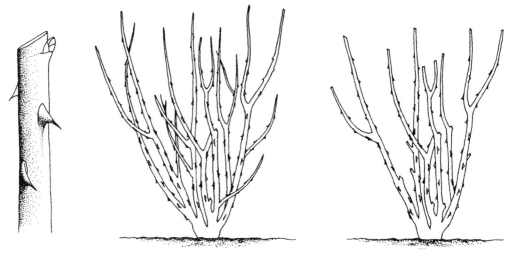

Correct pruning cut
above a bud

Bush rose before (left) and after pruning

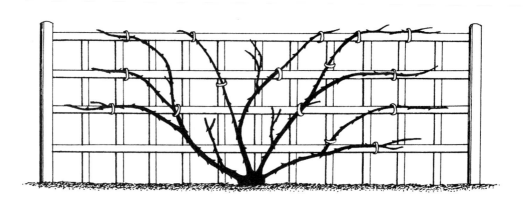

Correctly pruned and espaliered climber

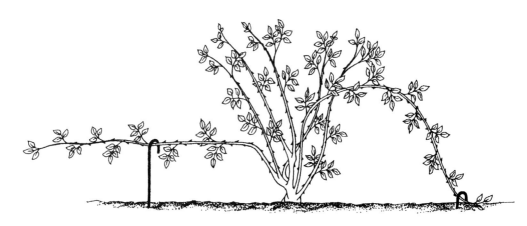

Shrub rose with branches pegged horizontally (left) and hooped (right)

164

draped effect, or it can be trimmed at pruning time to give a more formal-shaped hedge.

Neglected old roses, whether bush or climbers, can usually be rejuventated by pruning the old wood very hard to just above ground level. Roses treated like this will send out lots of new growth quite quickly, producing many flowers the following year. It is important to remember that many roses need to be three or four years old to provide the display of flowers they are capable of; the older and larger they get, the better the display. A fourteen-year-old bush of the Damask 'Ispahan' at Roseneath becomes a mound of flowers 2 m high and 4 m wide each spring.

Roses in containers should have their soil renewed every two or three years as it will become exhausted. At this time, give them a good hard prune. They should also be pruned well every winter, reducing the length by two-thirds to three-quarters and removing all old, diseased and twiggy wood.

After pruning has been completed, and the prunings and old leaves have been taken away and burned, a good spray with copper oxychloride and winter spraying oil will kill any spores of fungous diseases, scale and other nasties not eliminated by the lime sulphur sprayed two to three weeks earlier. As well, the copper and oil spray will seal any cuts and stop diseases from entering them. It is also advisable to spray the ground under the roses to complete the job.

Late winter is a good time to propagate roses from cuttings. Choose some of the previous season's wood; a stem with an old, dead flower or hip on it is ideal. Cut pieces about the length of a pencil, above the top eye and below the bottom one. Put the cuttings in the ground so half the length is buried, in a place where they can be watered and will get some sun during the summer months. Move them to a more permanent place in the next autumn-winter season. Some varieties are very easy to grow from cuttings; others are more difficult, but rooting hormones can help get these started. Layering is another method that can be quite successful. Peg the branch down and cover it with soil, leaving the tip exposed. It should be left like this until the following autumn, when, if it has rooted, it can be moved to a new position.

SPRING: FERTILISING, SPRAYING, DEAD-HEADING

As winter turns to spring, it's time to fertilise roses generously and mulch around the plants. Use an animal fertiliser at the rate of a large shovelful per square metre, but be careful when using fowl manure as it burns plants easily. Mulch such as sawdust, straw, bark, wood shavings, shredded leaves, mushroom compost or coffee grounds can be applied on top of this to suppress weeds and keep moisture in the ground; it can also help to break up heavy clay. Mulches require nitrogen as they decompose and can rob the plants of this vital element; additional animal manure will provide the extra nitrogen and prevent a deficiency. If you are using a balanced rose fertiliser or a general garden fertiliser, fork it into the soil before mulching. These fertilisers release their nutrients over a three-month period, building up to a peak after a month and then tailing off after two months. It is therefore best to apply them every two months from spring until autumn to get a constant supply of nutrients throughout the growing season. You may prefer to use more expensive but very reliable long-term, slow-release fertilisers such as Osmocote or Magamp; these need to be applied only once a year, in the spring. With all fertilisers, the idea is to keep the roses growing vigorously so that diseases can't catch up with the new growth.

A regular spraying programme will also keep diseases at bay. A two- to three-week interval between sprays is usually adequate. It is best to use up to three different sprays as pests and diseases can build up a resistance if sprays are used too often without a break. A good general systemic fungicide like Saprol or Bravo and a combination fungicide-insecticide like Super Shield or Guild can be used alternately. Preventive fungicides like the copper sprays are good for use at summer strength for black spot, downy mildew and rust. Spraying sulphur can be used if powdery mildew is a problem. These two sprays are not compatible with each other or with some of the more commonly used sprays, so follow instructions very carefully, always using gloves, a mask and goggles, and covering all exposed skin.

Two or three weeks after pruning, downy mildew may start to appear and can defoliate the plants very quickly. General symptoms are reddish tinges and a slight curling on the new leaves, followed by a reddish blotching on the leaves and stems of the branches. Ridomil is the best fungicide to use; Saprol, Bravo or copper oxychloride and cupric hydroxide will also bring it under control. It may be necessary to use one of these sprays every seven to fourteen days until the symptoms disappear and healthy new leaves appear.

Black spot is more prevalent later in the spring, with round black or brown spots surrounded by a yellow line appearing on the leaves. Rust may also be starting to show itself on the underside of the leaves at this time. The spores are small spots of yellow that turn to orange dust, and they can blow around and settle on and from other plants, not only roses.

Aphids are small sucking insects that can appear from spring to autumn. They usually gather on newly formed buds and shoots. You may also find caterpillars burrowing into and eating the new buds, but they are generally not a problem. Another small pest is the green beetle or shield bug, which is also a sap-sucker that is often to be found on roses. Most proprietary brands of general-purpose rose spray with a systemic action will kill these insects through the sap that they suck from the plant.

Remember that it's not essential to spray. Some roses are more prone to diseases and you may feel like evicting the culprit plant for a much more healthy variety. A few black spots will not kill your rose bush, and in these days when environmental and conservation issues are so much to the fore, we should use as few chemicals as possible. Companion plantings, for example pyrethrum daisies, garlic and chives, are all worth trying. Any insecticide will kill off beneficial predator insects like ladybirds and katydids as well as the undersirables, so leave the aphids and caterpillars to the birds, use your fingers if you have only a few roses, or hose them off your plants. You could try some natural sprays or remedies. Professor R. Kenneth Horst, author of *The Compendium of Rose Diseases* and the fifth edition of *Wescott's Plant Disease Handbook*, uses a mixture of three teaspoons of baking soda to a gallon of water and two and a half tablespoons of spraying oil to the gallon once a week to stop powdery mildew and black spot from becoming established on his plants. If you want perfect roses you must keep a regular spraying programme going. Your local nursery or garden centre is the best place to find out what pests and diseases are prevalent in your area and what is needed to combat them.

There are several viruses that affect roses, and some varieties will be infected with more than one. Petal fleck virus is easiest seen in pink or red flowers as short, deep-coloured lines running down the petals. It is not so easily seen in white, yellow or pale-coloured roses. Mosaic virus shows up in the leaves as a white or creamy yellow splashing or mottling. There is no effective cure for these virus diseases, so it is best to dig out the infected plant and burn it as the virus is present in the sap. Disinfect your spade and secateurs after digging out the plant and cutting it up. Some roots will probably be left behind in the soil so it is best not to plant another rose in this position for at least six months. Other garden plants like dahlias, chrysanthemums and nicotiana can also be infected with several varieties of virus, so it is best to use a strong disinfectant on your secateurs after pruning or dead-heading these.

In mid-spring your roses should be growing in the most boisterous fashion. The mulch on the garden will suppress most weeds but there are still some to be removed. A watch must be kept on companion plants that may be encroaching on small or newly planted roses, which need air movement and sunlight to get established and will sulk and become diseased if too crowded.

This is the time we have all been waiting for, when flowers start bursting out everywhere. Dead-heading is at its peak — a chore and a bore, but a job that is very necessary. When dead-heading, remove half the flower-stem when the flowers are finished on it; this will keep the bush compact and give the new flowers stronger stems. Don't dead-head once-flowering roses that produce good hips; there is nothing worse than seeing roses like 'Fritz Nobis' and 'Scharlachglut' stripped of their embryonic hips.

Now is the time to remove old wood from once-flowering roses as they finish blooming. Really old and untidy bushes can even be cut back to ground level and they will come away with lots of new growth, ready for next season's flowers. Spray with summer strength copper oxychloride to seal the cuts.

Any strong new growth appearing now should be staked, or tied to pergolas and fences to stop it from being broken or damaged. This new growth will produce next year's flowers. Any wood that is weak or not producing good blooms can be pruned out to encourage new growth.

After this main flush of flowers has ended, another side-dressing of general garden or rose fertiliser will keep the plant growing and healthy. If you have used long-term, slow-release fertiliser in early spring, this will not be necessary. Cuttings can also be taken at this time. You may be starting to water now if the season is dry, but remember that water will wash off sprays and encourages black spot and mildew, so keep it off the foliage as much as possible. Watering systems that direct water straight onto the ground are now available and are preferable for roses. It is better to give plants a good deep soaking once a week than to give frequent overhead sprinklings. Lighter soil will, of course, need watering more frequently.

SUMMER–EARLY AUTUMN: DEAD-HEADING, WATERING

Late spring and early summer are when most private and public gardens are at their best and many are open to visitors, and people are inspired to start buying roses with a vengeance. Container-grown roses can be planted all through the spring and summer months. At this time of the year try to plant on a cool day or at the end of the day. Dig a hole large enough to hold the ball of roots and fork a handful of long-term fertiliser into the subsoil. Make a mound of soil in the hole and open up the root ball from the base of the plant, gently shaking off some of the mix, and spread the roots into the hole and over the mound. Now spread the soil back over the roots and cover with topsoil, lightly treading around the plant. Water in well and keep staked. Misting occasionally during the first few days will help the plant to get established; do not let it dry out.

From mid- to late summer watering is essential; if you can't water, it is a good idea to lightly fluff up the soil with a fork as a hard-baked soil will dry out very quickly. Take care not to get too close to the plant and accidentally lift it. A topping up of mulch is also helpful now, particularly if you have been disturbing the roots of plants by cultivating around them.

Powdery mildew can occur again at this time, especially on some of the small Polyantha Roses, and Karathane or spraying sulphur can be used to control it. Red mite can be a problem in hot dry weather. The leaves appear dusty and dull, and the silver-grey underside is damaged by the sucking of these very small spider-like, red-spotted green mites that are protecting themselves with a fine webbing. Spraying with a good miticide two or three times a season should keep them at bay. When watering, a regular blast from the hose on the underside of the leaves also helps to discourage them.

Scale can also appear in summer, usually on older wood down near the base of the plant, although it will usually have been killed in winter with the lime sulphur and oil spray. The more common type appears on the stem and can, quite quickly, become massed together among the thorns as small white dots. There is a larger type that is usually brown and much more solitary. An easy way of getting rid of scale is to mix, in a small jar, spraying oil at winter strength with a small amount of Maldison (according to instructions on the label), and paint this on to the infected stem with a small paintbrush or old toothbrush.

In late summer you should be getting good repeat flushes of flowers so you'll need to keep dead-heading, particularly some of the Teas and their hybrids, which can keep flowering into winter in warmer climates. Many repeat-flowering roses, for example 'Dainty Bess', also produce good rose hips in the autumn. If you want this display instead of more flowers, you must stop dead-heading them from mid- to late summer.

The last side-dressing of fertiliser should be put on the garden now with a light dressing of potash a few weeks later. This will help to harden the last new growth. In climates with heavy frosts and snow, dead-heading should be stopped in mid-autumn in order to slow down their growth. This is a good time to apply lime (at the rate of 60–120 grams per square metre), as the winter rains will wash it into the soil. Basic slag can also be applied now. This is a good way of providing calcium, phosphorus and many trace elements to the soil. It is slow-acting, building up the soil's fertility and structure, making clay soils more crumbly and easier to work. Apply approximately 90–180 grams per square metre depending on the pH. It is advisable to check this with a testing kit from a garden centre. The pH should be 7, which is just on the limey side of neutral.

APPENDIX

Annotated list of species and hybrids

The following list includes a brief summary of all the roses found in the text as well as many others, old-fashioned and modern, which are suitable for gardens incorporating old roses. Date of introduction, type, flower shape and colour, fruit, fragrance, hips and flowering habit are included for each rose.

'À Longs Pédoncules', 1854, Moss, double soft pink, fragrant, early summer.

'Abbotswood', 1954, Hybrid Canina, loose double pink, scented, spring.

'Abraham Darby', 1985, English, shrub/climber, large double apricot, very fragrant, continuous.

'Achievement', 1925, Hybrid Wichuraiana, variegated foliage, clusters, small double rose-pink, summer.

'Adam', 1833, Tea, double soft salmon-apricot, scented, continuous.

'Adam Messerich', 1920, Bourbon, loosely double mid-pink, fragrant, continuous.

'Adam Rackles', 1905, Hybrid Tea, large marbled pink and white, scented, recurrent.

'Adélaide d'Orléans', 1926, Hybrid Sempervirens, clusters, semi-double creamy buff, early summer.

'Agathe Incarnata', 1800, Gallica, very double soft pink, early summer.

'Aglaia', 1896, Multiflora Rambler, small semi-double soft yellow, thornless, scented, spring.

'Agnes', 1922, Hybrid Rugosa, double buff-yellow, scented, recurrent.

'Aimée Vibert', 1828, Noisette, clusters, very double white, scented, late summer.

'Akashi', 1968, ground-cover, medium pink rosettes, continuous.

'Alain Blanchard', 1839, Gallica, single deep red with purple flecks, scented, early summer.

'Albéric Barbier', 1900, Hybrid Wichuraiana, double creamy white, apple scented, recurrent.

'Albertine', 1921, Hybrid Wichuraiana, loosely double apricot-pink, fragrant, early summer.

'Alchemist', 1956, climber, very double buff-apricot, fragrant, spring.

'Alister Stella Gray', 1894, Noisette, clusters, small double yellow, scented, continuous.

'Aloha', 1949, shrub/climber, large double rose-pink, fragrant, continuous.

'Altissimo', 1967, climber, clusters, single red, continuous.

'Amadis', 1829, Boursault, double warm pink, recurrent.

'American Pillar', 1909, Hybrid Wichuraiana, single light red with a white eye, summer.

'Anaïs Ségales', 1837, Gallica, double mauve-purple, scented, spring.

'Andenken an Alma de l'Aigle', 1896, Hybrid Musk, loose double mid-pink, scented, continuous.

'Anemone Rose', 1895, Hybrid Laevigata (*Rosa* x *anemonoides*), large single pink, scented, recurrent.

'Angel Face', 1968, Floribunda, double rich mauve-lilac, fragrant, continuous.

'Anna Maria de Montravel', 1880, Chinensis, clusters, small double white, continuous.

'Anna Oliver', 1872, Tea, double creamy apricot, scented, continuous.

'Anna Pavlova', 1981, Hybrid Tea, double silver-pink, very fragrant, continuous.

'Anne Endt', unknown, Hybrid Foliolosa, single magenta, hips, scented, recurrent.

'Apple Blossom', 1932, Multiflora Rambler, clusters, single pink, scented, spring.

'Applejack', 1973, shrub, semi-double, pink, fragrant, recurrent.

'Archiduc Joseph', 1872, Tea, very double salmon-pink, fragrant, continuous.

'Arthur Bell', 1965, Floribunda, double rich yellow, fragrant, continuous.

'Arthur de Sansal', 1855, Portland, double reddish purple, fragrant, recurrent.

'Autumnalis', unknown, Hybrid Moschata, small loosely double palest yellow, scented, recurrent.

'Avalanche', 1989, Floribunda, double creamy white, continuous.

'Aviateur Blériot', 1910, Wichuraiana Rambler, clusters, small apricot-yellow, early summer.

'Ballerina', 1937, Hybrid Musk, clusters, single pink, hips, light scent, continuous.

'Banksia Hybride di Castello', 1920, Hybrid Banksia, double white, scented, recurrent.

'Banksia Purezza', 1961, Hybrid Banksia, clusters, double white, very fragrant, recurrent.

'Bantry Bay', 1967, climber, semi-double mid-pink, continuous.

'Baron Girod l'Ain', 1897, Hybrid Perpetual, double red edged white, recurrent.

'Baroness Rothschild', 1868, Hybrid Perpetual, large double pale pink, scented, recurrent.

'Baronne Prévost', 1842, Hybrid Perpetual, large double rose-pink, very fragrant, recurrent.

'Belle Amour', unknown, Alba, double soft salmon-pink, scented, summer.

'Belle de Crécy', pre-1840, Gallica, double lavender-purple, scented, summer.

'Belle Isis', 1845, Gallica, very double palest pink, very fragrant, spring.

'Belle Poitevine', 1894, Hybrid Rugosa, semi-double cerise-pink, hips, scented, recurrent.

'Black Boy', 1919, climber, double dark red, fragrant, summer.

'Blairii No. 2', 1845, climbing Bourbon, double soft pink, fragrant, recurrent.

'Blanc de Vibert', 1847, Portland, double white, recurrent.

'Blanc Double de Coubert', 1892, Hybrid Rugosa, semi-double pure white, scented, continuous.

'Bleu Magenta', 1900, Multiflora Rambler, clusters, small double violet-purple, spring.

'Bloomfield Abundance', 1920, Polyantha, small, pale pink, fragrant, recurrent.

'Bloomfield Courage', 1925, rambler, clusters, single red, early summer.

'Bloomfield Dainty', 1924, Hybrid Musk, single yellow, scented, continuous.

'Blush Noisette', 1825, Noisette, clusters, semi-double soft lavender-pink from deep pink buds, clove fragrance, continuous.

'Blush Rambler', 1903, Multiflora Rambler, clusters, semi-double soft pink, scented, late spring-early summer.

'Bobbie James', 1961, Multiflora Rambler, clusters, semi-double white, scented, spring.

'Bon Silène', 1839, Tea, double warm red, scented, continuous.

'Botzaris', 1856, Damask, very double white, scented, late spring.

'Boule de Neige', 1867, Bourbon, double white with button eye, fragrant, continuous.

'Bourbon Queen', 1837, Bourbon, loosely double large rose-pink, scented, spring.

'Bredon', 1984, English, shrub, double soft buff-apricot, scented, continuous.

'Buff Beauty', 1939, Hybrid Musk, double buff-yellow, fragrant, continuous.

'Bullata', pre-1600, Centifolia, very double warm pink, unusual foliage, scented, late spring.

'Calocarpa', pre-1891, Hybrid Rugosa, single cerise-pink, hips, fragrant, recurrent.

'Cameo', 1932, Polyantha, clusters, small double salmon, continuous.

'Canary Bird', 1908, Hybrid Xanthina, single yellow, fragrant, spring.

'Cardinal de Richelieu', 1840, Gallica, very double burgundy, scented, spring.

'Cardinal Hume', 1984, shrub, clusters, semi-double purple, perfumed, continuous.

'Catherine Mermet', 1869, Tea, semi-double lavender-pink, scented, continuous.

'Cécile Brunner', 1881, Chinensis, small pale pink, scented, continuous.

—— 1904, climber, small pale pink, scented, recurrent.

'Celestial', 'Céleste', ancient, Alba, double soft pink, fragrant, spring.

'Céline Forestier', 1842, Noisette, very double soft lemon, fragrant, continuous.

'Celsiana', pre-1750, Damask, large semi-double soft pink, fragrant, spring.

'Cerise Bouquet', 1958, Hybrid Multibracteata, double cerise-pink, scented, late spring.

'Champneys' Pink Cluster', 1802, Noisette, clusters, small soft pink, fragrant, recurrent.

'Chapeau de Napoléon', 'Crested Moss', 1826, Centifolia, very double pink, fragrant, spring.

'Charles Albanel', 1980, Hybrid Rugosa, semi-double mid-pink, hips, fragrant, continuous.

'Charles Austin', 1973, English, shrub/climber, very double apricot, fragrant, recurrent.

'Charles de Mills', pre-1840, Gallica, very double purple-crimson, scented, spring.

'Château de Clos Vougeot', 1908, Hybrid Perpetual, double dark red, fragrant, recurrent.

'Chaucer', 1970, English, shrub, loosely double mid-pink, fragrant, continuous.

'Cherokee Latham', unknown, climber, large single pink, hips, spring.

'Chianti', 1967, English, shrub, double purple-crimson, scented, spring.

'Chloris', ancient, Alba, double softest pink, thornless, fragrant, spring.

'Clair Matin', 1960, shrub/climber, semi-double salmon-pink, continuous.

'Claire Jacquier', 1888, Noisette, clusters, yellow to pale yellow, scented, spring.

'Cloth of Gold', 1843, Noisette, large double butter-yellow, fragrant, continuous.

'Cocktail', 1959, shrub, single bright red with yellow eye, continuous.

'Commandant Beaurepaire', 1874, Bourbon, double striped crimson-red-pink-white, fragrant, recurrent.

'Complicata', unknown, Gallica, single deep rose-pink, hips, spring.

'Comte de Chambord', 1860, Portland, double dark

pink, very fragrant, continuous.

'Comtesse du Cayla', 1902, Hybrid Chinensis, double pink-apricot-orange-red, fragrant, continuous.

'Conchita', 1935, Polyantha, clusters, small double salmon-apricot, continuous.

'Conditorum', ancient, Gallica, double rich red, scented, late spring.

'Constance Spry', 1960, shrub/climber, large loosely double mid-pink, scented, spring.

'Copper Glow', unknown, climber, double salmon-orange, fragrant, late spring.

'Cornelia', 1925, Hybrid Musk, clusters, small double salmon-pink, fragrant, continuous.

'Corylus', 1988, Hybrid Rugosa, single silver-pink, scented, continuous.

'Cramoisi Picoté', 1834, Gallica, very double light red with darker markings, scented, spring.

'Crépuscule', 1904, Noisette, clusters, double apricot, scented, continuous.

'Crimson Glory', 1935, Hybrid Tea, very double deep red, very fragrant, continuous.

—— 1946, climbing Hybrid Tea, very double deep red, very fragrant, late spring.

'Crimson Showers', 1951, Hybrid Wichuraiana, small double red rosettes, scented, early summer.

'Cupid', 1915, climbing Hybrid Tea, single soft silver-pink, scented, spring.

'Cymbeline', 1982, English, shrub/climber, fully double pale greyish pink, scented, recurrent.

'D'Aguesseau', 1837, Gallica, very double crimson, scented, spring.

'Dainty Bess', 1925, Hybrid Tea, single strawberry-pink, hips, tea scented, continuous.

—— 1935, climbing Hybrid Tea, single strawberry-pink, hips, tea scented, continuous.

'Dainty Maid', 1940, Floribunda, single rose-pink, scented, continuous.

'Danaë', 1913, Hybrid Musk, semi-double cream, scented, continuous.

'Danse de Feu', 1953, Floribunda climber, clusters, double vivid scarlet becoming purple, continuous.

'Dapple Dawn', 1983, English, shrub, single warm pink, hips, continuous.

'Dawning', unknown, climber, loose double mid-pink, scented, continuous.

'De la Grifferaie', 1845, Hybrid Multiflora, very double mauve-pink, very fragrant, spring.

'Desprez à Fleurs Jaunes', 1830, Noisette, double peachy yellow, very fragrant, continuous.

'Devoniensis', 1858, climbing Tea, loose double creamy white blushed pink, fragrant, spring.

'Donna Maria', unknown, rambler, clusters, double white, thornless, scented, late spring.

'Dorothy Perkins', 1902, Hybrid Wichuraiana, large clusters, small double pink, summer.

'Dortmund', 1955, shrub/climber, single bright red with white eye, continuous.

'Double Cream', Hybrid Pimpinellifolia, small double cream, hips, spring.

'Double Pink', Hybrid Pimpinellifolia, small double pink, hips, spring.

'Dr W. van Fleet', 1910, Hybrid Wichuraiana, double soft pink, fragrant, spring.

'Dublin Bay', 1976, climber, clusters, double rich red, continuous.

'Duchesse d'Angoulême', 1838, Gallica, double soft pink, scented, spring.

'Duchesse de Brabant', 1857, Tea, loose double pink, scented, continuous.

'Duchesse de Montebello', pre-1850, Gallica, very double pale pink, fragrant, spring.

'Duke of Edinburgh', 1868, Hybrid Perpetual, double dark red, scented, recurrent.

'Dundee Rambler', c. 1850, rambler, double milky white, musk scent, spring.

'Dunwich Rose', unknown, Hybrid Pimpinellifolia, small single cream, soft scent, summer.

'Easlea's Golden Rambler', 1932, rambler, double butter-yellow, fragrant, summer.

'Ellen Willmott', 1936, Hybrid Tea, single cream flushed pink, scented, continuous.

'Elmshorn', 1951, shrub/climber, clusters, small cherry-red, continuous.

'Emily Gray', 1918, Hybrid Wichuraiana, double copper-yellow, scented, spring.

'Empress Josephine', pre-1850, Gallica, large loose double lavender-pink, scented, spring.

'Ena Harkness', 1946, Hybrid Tea, double red, very fragrant, continuous.

—— 1954, climbing Hybrid Tea, double red, very fragrant, summer.

'English Garden', 1987, English, shrub, fully double soft buff-yellow, scented, continuous.

'Erfurt', 1939, shrub, single clear rich pink, pale white in the centre, yellow stamens, continuous.

'Étoile de Hollande', 1919, Hybrid Tea, loose double rich deep red, very fragrant, recurrent.

—— 1931, climbing Hybrid Tea, loose double rich deep red, very fragrant, recurrent.

'Eugénie Guinoisseau', 1864, Moss, double crimson-purple, scented, recurrent.

'Eva', 1933, Hybrid Musk, clusters, single red, scented, continuous.

'Excelsa', 1900, Hybrid Wichuraiana, clusters, small red double, summer.

'Eyeopener', 1989, ground-cover, single scarlet, continuous.

'Fabvier', 1832, Chinensis, loose scarlet, continuous.

'Fair Bianca', 1982, English, shrub, very double large white, fragrant, continuous.

'Fairyland', 1980, ground-cover, small double soft pink, continuous.

'Fantin-Latour', unknown, Centifolia, double soft pink, fragrant, late spring.

'Felicia', 1928, Hybrid Musk, loose double pale apricot-pink, fragrant, continuous.

'Félicité et Perpétue', 1827, Hybrid Sempervirens, clusters, small white rosettes, fragrant, late spring.

'Félicité Parmentier', 1834, Alba, very double soft pink, fragrant, spring.

'Fellemberg', 1857, Hybrid Chinensis, double lavender-red, continuous.

'Ferdinand Pichard', 1921, Hybrid Perpetual, loose double striped white-pink-red, fragrant, recurrent.

'Fimbriata', 1891, Hybrid Rugosa, small blush white, recurrent.

'F. J. Grootendorst', 1918, Hybrid Rugosa, clusters, small double red, continuous.

'Francesca', 1928, Hybrid Musk, loose double soft yellow, fragrant, continuous.

'Francis Dubreuil', 1894, Tea, loose double deep red, very fragrant, continuous.

'Francis E. Lester', 1946, Hybrid Multiflora, clusters, single blush white, hips, fragrant, late spring.

'François Juranville', 1906, Hybrid Wichuraiana, double pale apricot-pink, fragrant, spring.

'Frau Dagmar Hastrup', 1914, Hybrid Rugosa, single silver-pink, hips, fragrant, continuous.

'Frau Karl Druschki', 1901, Hybrid Perpetual, large double white, recurrent.

'Fred Loads', 1968, shrub/climber, clusters, semi-double apricot-pink, continuous.

'Fred Streeter', 1951, Hybrid Moyesii, single rose-pink, hips, scented, late spring.

'Frensham', 1946, Floribunda, clusters, semi-double red, continuous.

'Fritz Nobis', 1940, shrub, loose double soft pink, hips, scented, spring.

'Frühlingsanfang', 1950, Hybrid Pimpinellifolia, single white, hips, fragrant, late spring.

'Frühlingsduft', 1949, Hybrid Pimpinellifolia, very double soft yellow, very fragrant, late spring.

'Frühlingsgold', 1937, Hybrid Pimpinellifolia, single yellow, fragrant, spring.

'Frühlingsmorgen', 1942, Hybrid Pimpinellifolia, single pink, hips, fragrant, recurrent.

'Gardenia', 1899, Hybrid Wichuraiana, clusters, double pale yellow, fragrant, late spring.

'Général Galliéni', 1899, Tea, double buff to red, scented, continuous.

'Général Kléber', 1856, Moss, double bright pink, very fragrant, late spring.

'Général Schablikine', 1878, Tea, double pink-salmon tones, scented, continuous.

'Geranium', 1938, Hybrid Moyesii, single bright red, hips, late spring.

'Gerbe Rose', 1904, Hybrid Wichuraiana, double soft pink, scented, recurrent.

'Gertrude Jekyll', 1987, English, shrub, very double rich rose-pink, very fragrant, continuous.

'Ghislaine de Féligonde', 1916, Hybrid Multiflora, double soft apricot, fragrant, recurrent.

'Gloire de Dijon', 1853, Noisette, very double soft apricot, fragrant, continuous.

'Gloire de France', 1819, Gallica, double soft pink with darker tones, fragrant, spring.

'Gloire de Guilan', 1849, Damask, double pale pink, fragrant, spring.

'Gloire Lyonnaise', 1885, Hybrid Perpetual, semi-double creamy white, scented, recurrent.

'Gloria Mundi', 1929, Polyantha, small orange-red cupped, continuous.

'Golden Moss', 1932, Moss, double cupped soft yellow, scented, summer.

'Golden Ophelia', 1918, climber, double buff-apricot-yellow, fragrant, recurrent.

'Golden Salmon', 1926, Polyantha, small cupped salmon-orange, continuous.

'Golden Showers', 1956, climber, large double bright yellow, scented, continuous.

'Golden Wings', 1953, shrub/climber, single mid-yellow, scented, continuous.

'Goldfinch', 1907, Hybrid Multiflora, semi-double soft yellow, scented, early spring.

'Gracilis', unknown, Boursault, loosely double rose-pink, spring.

'Graham Thomas', 1983, English, shrub/climber, large double glowing yellow, fragrant, continuous.

'Grandchild', modern, Hybrid Chinensis, small double pink, scented, continuous.

'Great Western', 1840, Bourbon, double red, fragrant, summer.

'Green Ice', 1971, miniature, pale greenish rosettes with pink flush, continuous.

'Gruss an Aachen', 1909, shrub, very double soft creamy apricot, fragrant, continuous.

'Gruss an Coburg', 1927, Hybrid Tea, double copper-apricot, scented, continuous.

'Gruss en Teplitz', 1897, Hybrid Chinensis, double cerise-red, fragrant, continuous.

'Guinée', 1938, climbing Hybrid Tea, very double dark red, fragrant, recurrent.

'Gustav Grunewald', 1903, Hybrid Tea, double pink, very fragrant, continuous.

'Handel', 1965, Floribunda climber, double white with dark pink edges, continuous.

'Hansa', 1905, Rugosa, loosely double cerise-red, hips, fragrant, recurrent.

'Hebe's Lip', 1912, Hybrid Eglantine, semi-double white touched red, very fragrant, late spring.

'Henry Hudson', Hybrid Rugosa, semi-double white, hips, fragrant, recurrent.

'Heritage', 1984, English, shrub, double cupped soft pink, fragrant, continuous.

'Hermosa', 1840, China, double lavender-pink, scented, continuous.

'Highdownensis', 1928, Hybrid Moyesii, single bright cerise-pink, hips, late spring.

'Hilda Murrell', 1984, shrub, very double bright pink, scented, recurrent.

'Hippolyte', 1800, Gallica, very double purple-red, fragrant, spring.

'Honorine de Brabant', unknown, Bourbon, double striped white-mauve-pink, fragrant, recurrent.

'Horstmann's Rosenresli', 1955, Floribunda, double white, scented, continuous.

'Hume's Blush', 1810, China, semi-double soft salmon-pink, tea scented, continuous.

'Iceberg', 1958, Floribunda, clusters, semi-double white, scented, continuous.

—— 1968, climbing Floribunda, clusters, semi-double white, scented, continuous.

'Indica Major', unknown, Hybrid Chinensis, double white to pale pink, early spring.

'Ispahan', pre-1830, Damask, double warm soft pink, fragrant, late spring.

'Jacques Cartier', 1868, Portland, fully double light pink, deeper in the centre, fragrant, continuous.

'Jaquenetta', 1983, English, shrub, semi-double apricot, continuous.

'Jean Ducher', 1873, Tea, double globular soft creamy coral-pink, fragrant, continuous.

'Jersey Beauty', 1899, Hybrid Wichuraiana, single pale yellow, scented, late spring.

'Josephine Bruce', 1949, Hybrid Tea, double deep red, fragrant, continuous.

—— 1954, climbing Hybrid Tea, double deep red, fragrant, recurrent.

'Joseph's Coat', 1964, shrub/climber, loose double orange-yellow to red, continuous.

'Julia's Rose', 1976, Hybrid Tea, double burnished brown, scented, continuous.

'Juno', 1832, Centifolia, very double soft pink, fragrant, late spring.

'Karlsruhe', 1950, Hybrid Kordesii, very double bright pink, scented, continuous.

'Katharina Zeimet', 1901, Polyantha, clusters, small double white, scented, continuous.

'Kathleen', 1922, Hybrid Musk, clusters, single mid-pink, hips, scented, continuous.

'Kathleen Harrop', 1919, Bourbon, loose double soft pink, very fragrant, continuous.

'Kiftsgate', 1954, Filipes, large clusters, single white, hips, fragrant, late spring.

'Kirsten Poulsen', 1924, Hybrid Polyantha, clusters, single red, continuous.

'Königin von Dänemark', 1826, Alba, very double soft to mid-pink, fragrant, spring.

'La Belle Distinguée', unknown, Hybrid Eglantine, double purple, fragrant, late spring.

'La Belle Sultane', *R. gallica violacea*, very ancient, Gallica, single burgundy, perfumed, spring.

'La France', 1867, Hybrid Tea, double silver-pink, scented, continuous.

'La Noblesse', 1856, Centifolia, very double pale pink, fragrant, recurrent.

'La Reine', 1842, Hybrid Perpetual, large fully petalled rose-pink, fragrant, recurrent.

'La Reine Victoria', 1872, Bourbon, double cupped rose-pink, fragrant, continuous.

'La Rubanée', 'Village Maid', 1845, Centifolia, double striped off-white-pink, scented, late spring.

'La Ville de Bruxelles', 1849, Damask, very double bright rose-pink, fragrant, spring.

'Lady Alice Stanley', 1909, Hybrid Tea, double pink with deeper reverse, scented, continuous.

'Lady Hillingdon', 1910, Tea, double apricot-yellow, fragrant, continuous.

—— 1917, climbing Tea, double apricot-yellow, fragrant, continuous.

'Lady Mary Fitzwilliam', 1882, Hybrid Tea, double pink, fragrant, continuous.

'Lady Sylvia', 1926, Hybrid Tea, double soft pink, fragrant, continuous.

'Lady Waterlow', 1903, climbing Hybrid Tea, loose double warm pink, scented, continuous.

'Lamarque', 1830, Noisette, very double white, very fragrant, continuous.

'Lauré Davoust', 1842, rambler, clusters, small lavender-pink rosettes, recurrent.

'Lavender Dream', 1984, shrub, clusters, semi-double, lavender-pink.

'Lavender Lassie', 1959, Hybrid Musk, clusters, double warm lavender-pink, very fragrant, continuous.

'Lawrence Johnston', 1923, climber, almost single bright yellow, perfumed, recurrent.

'Le Rêve', 1920, Hybrid Foetida, semi-double yellow, very fragrant, recurrent.

'Leander', 1982, English, clusters, double apricot, fragrant, recurrent.

'Leda', pre-1900, Damask, very double white edged red, fragrant, late spring.

'Leverkusen', 1954, climber, double soft yellow, scented, recurrent.

'Lilian Austin', 1973, English, shrub, double copper-pink, fragrant, recurrent.

'Little Gem', 1880, Moss, double mid-pink, scented, late spring.

'Little White Pet', 1879, Wichuraiana sport, clusters, small white rosettes, scented, continuous.

'Lorraine Lee', 1924, climbing Hybrid Tea, loose double warm pink, fragrant, continuous.

'Louis XIV', 1859, China, double black-red, light scent, continuous.

'Louise Odier', 1851, Bourbon, very double cupped warm pink, fragrant, continuous.

'Lucetta', 1983, English, shrub/climber, large loose double pale pink, fragrant, continuous.

'Maiden's Blush', pre-1500, Alba, very double soft pink, fragrant, late spring.

'Maigold', 1953, climber, semi-double deep rich yellow, fragrant, early spring, sometimes repeats.

'Maman Cochet', 1893, Tea, double soft pink, fragrant, continuous.

'Maréchel Niel', 1864, Noisette, double butter-yellow, fragrant, recurrent.

'Margaret Merril', 1977, Floribunda, double white blushed pink, fragrant, continuous.

'Maria's Rose', 1990, shrub, large very pale pink, fragrant, continuous.

'Marie de Blois', 1852, Moss, very double cerise-pink, fragrant, recurrent.

'Marie Louise', 1813, Damask, double soft pink, fragrant, spring.

'Marie Parvie', 1888, Polyantha, small double soft pink, continuous.

'Marie van Houtte', 1871, climbing Tea, very pale yellow tinged red, scented, recurrent.

'Marjorie Fair', 1978, shrub, clusters, single red, continuous.

'Martin Frobisher', 1968, Hybrid Rugosa, loose double soft pink, scented, recurrent.

'Mary Rose', 1983, English, shrub, large mid-pink, fragrant, continuous.

'Mary Wallace', 1924, Hybrid Wichuraiana, semi-double rose-pink, fragrant, spring.

'Mary Webb', 1984, English, shrub, double soft yellow, strongly fragrant, recurrent.

'Maxima', pre-1400, Alba, double white, fragrant, spring.

'May Queen', 1898, Hybrid Wichuraiana, double pale pink, scented, recurrent.

'Meg', 1954, climber, semi-double large apricot, hips, scented, spring.

'Mermaid', 1917, Hybrid Bracteata, large single soft creamy yellow, evergreen, fragrant, continuous.

'Mev. G. A. van Rossen', 1922, climbing Hybrid Tea, large double buff-yellow, scented, recurrent.

'Michèle Meilland', 1945, Hybrid Tea, double soft apricot-pink, fragrant, continuous.

—— 1945, climbing Hybrid Tea, double soft apricot-pink, fragrant, recurrent.

'Mignonette', 1880, Polyantha, clusters, small double softest pink, continuous.

'Milky Way', unknown, rambler, clusters, semi-double creamy yellow, hips, scented, late spring.

'Minnehaha', 1905, Hybrid Wichuraiana, pale pink rosettes, late spring.

'Miss Muffet', 1989, rambler, clusters, semi-double scarlet, late spring.

'Mme Abel Chatenay', 1895, Hybrid Tea, double warm pink, fragrant, continuous.

'Mme Alfred Carrière', 1879, Noisette, loose double white blushed pink, fragrant, continuous.

'Mme Alice Garnier', 1906, Hybrid Wichuraiana, clusters, double apricot, scented, late spring.

'Mme Berkeley', 1809, Tea, double pale salmon-pink, scented, continuous.

'Mme Butterfly', 1918, Hybrid Tea, double soft pink with pale yellow tones, very fragrant, continuous.

'Mme Caroline Testout', 1890, climbing Hybrid Tea, double globular glowing pink, scented, continuous.

'Mme Charles', 1864, Tea, clusters, semi-double soft pink, scented, continuous.

'Mme Édouard Herriot', 'Daily Mail Rose', 1913, Hybrid Tea, double apricot, fragrant, recurrent.

—— 1921, climbing Hybrid Tea, fragrant, summer.

'Mme Ernst Calvat', 1888, Bourbon, large double warm pink, very fragrant, continuous.

'Mme Franziska Kruger', 1880, Tea, very double yellow with reddish flush, scented, continuous.

'Mme Georges Bruant', 1887, Hybrid Rugosa, semi-double white, fragrant, recurrent.

'Mme Grégoire Staechelin', 'Spanish Beauty', 1927, climbing Hybrid Tea, loose double silver-pink, hips, very fragrant, spring.

'Mme Hardy', 1832, Damask, very double white with button eye, very fragrant, spring.

'Mme Isaac Pereire', 1881, Bourbon, large double cerise-pink, very fragrant, continuous.

'Mme Jules Gravereaux', 1901, climbing Hybrid Tea, double apricot, fragrant, continuous.

'Mme Knorr', 1855, Portland, semi-double, deep rose-pink, scented, recurrent.

'Mme Laurette Messimy', 1887, China, clusters, loose double pink, continuous.

'Mme Lauriol de Barny', 1868, Bourbon, double pink, fragrant, recurrent.

'Mme Legras de St Germain', 1846, Alba, very double large white, fragrant, spring.

'Mme Louis Lévêque', 1874, Moss, double silver-pink, fragrant, recurrent.

'Mme P. S. Dupont', 1933, climbing Hybrid Tea, double butter-yellow, scented, recurrent.

'Mme Pierre Oger', 1874, Bourbon, double cupped cream to pink, fragrant, recurrent.

'Mme Plantier', 1835, Alba, shrub/pillar, double white, fragrant, late spring.

'Mme Sancy de Parabère', 1874, Boursault, double deep pink, thornless, late spring.

'Mme Victor Verdier', 1863, Hybrid Perpetual, large double crimson-red, fragrant, recurrent.

'Mme Wagram', 1895, Tea, very double soft silver-pink, scented, continuous.

'Mme Zoetmans', 1830, Damask, very double creamy white, fragrant, spring.

'Monsieur Tillier', 1891, Tea, semi-double red with violet tones, perfumed, continuous.

'Moonlight', 1913, Hybrid Musk, semi-double white, scented, continuous.

'Mozart', 1937, Hybrid Musk, clusters, single red, hips, scented, continuous.

'Mrs B. R. Cant', 1901, Hybrid Tea, very double bright pink, scented, continuous.

'Mrs Bosanquet', pre-1860, Hybrid Chinensis, double creamy white tinged red, scented, continuous.

'Mrs F. F. Prentice', 1925, Hybrid Perpetual, semi-double rose-pink, recurrent.

'Mrs Herbert Stevens', 1910, Hybrid Tea, double pure white, fragrant, recurrent.

—— 1922, climbing Hybrid Tea, double pure white, fragrant, recurrent.

'Mrs Inge Poulsen', 1952, Floribunda, clusters, soft apricot-pink, continuous.

'Mrs John Laing', 1887, Hybrid Perpetual, large double silver-pink, fragrant, recurrent.

'Mrs Merrilees', modern, Polyantha, clusters, small single pink with white eye, continuous.

'Mrs Oakley Fisher', 1921, Hybrid Tea, single apricot-yellow, scented, continuous.

'Mrs R. M. Finch', 1923, Polyantha, clusters, semi-double warm pink, continuous.

'Mutabilis', pre-1890, Chinensis, single apricot to rose-pink, continuous.

'Muttertag', 1950, Paree, clusters, double cupped red, continuous.

'Nancy Hayward', 1937, climber, single light red, continuous.

'Nancy Steen', 1976, shrub, double soft pink, scented, continuous.

'Nevada', 1927, Hybrid Moyesii, large single creamy white, recurrent.

'New Dawn', 1930, Hybrid Wichuraiana, loose double soft pink, scented, recurrent.

'Nightfall', Floribunda, double lilac-mauve, continuous.

'Niphetos', 1843, Tea, double white, fragrant, recurrent.

—— 1889, climbing Tea, double white, fragrant, recurrent.

'Nozomi', 1968, ground-cover, small single pink, spring.

'Nuits de Young', 1845, Moss, double purple-red, fragrant, spring.

'Oeillet Parfait', 1841, Gallica, double white striped red, scented, late spring.

'Old Blush China', pre-1750, loose double mid-pink, continuous.

'Omar Khayyàm', ancient, Damask, double warm pink,

fragrant, late spring.

'Ophelia', 1912, Hybrid Tea, double palest pink, fragrant, continuous.

—— 1920, climbing Hybrid Tea, double palest pink, fragrant, continuous.

'Papa Gontier', 1883, Hybrid Tea, double bright pink, scented, continuous.

'Papa Meilland', 1963, Hybrid Tea, large double dark red, very fragrant, recurrent.

'Parade', 1967, climber, double cerise-pink, scented, continuous.

'Parfum de l'Hay', 1901, Hybrid Rugosa, double cerise-red, very fragrant, recurrent.

'Parkdirektor Riggers', 1957, climber, almost single sharp red, continuous.

'Paul Crampel', 1930, Polyantha, clusters, geranium-red, continuous.

'Paul Neyron', 1869, Hybrid Perpetual, large double bright pink, scented, recurrent.

'Paul Transon', 1900, Hybrid Wichuraiana, very double apricot-pink, very fragrant, recurrent.

'Paul's Himalayan Musk', c. 1890, Hybrid Musk, clusters, double soft pink, scented, late spring.

'Paul's Lemon Pillar', 1915, climbing Hybrid Tea, very large double creamy white, hips, scented, spring.

'Paul's Scarlet', 1931, climber, clusters, light red, recurrent.

'Pax', 1918, Hybrid Musk, loose double white, scented, continuous.

'Peace', 1945, Hybrid Tea, large double soft lemon tinged pink, scented, continuous.

'Pearl Drift', 1980, shrub, clusters, single softest pink, scented, continuous.

'Penelope', 1924, Hybrid Musk, semi-double creamy apricot, scented, continuous.

'Perdita', 1983, English, shrub, double soft apricot-pink, scented, recurrent.

'Perla de Montserrat', 1945, miniature, clusters, double light pink, continuous.

'Perle des Blanches', unknown, Noisette, clusters, double white, scented, recurrent.

'Perle d'Or', 1894, Chinensis, clusters, small double apricot, continuous.

✓'Phyllis Bide', 1923, climber, clusters, apricot-yellow flushed pink, recurrent.

'Pink Bells', 1983, miniature, ground-cover, clusters, double warm pink, continuous.

'Pink Grootendorst', 1923, Hybrid Rugosa, clusters, carnation-shaped warm pink, continuous.

✓'Pink Perpétue', 1965, climber, double cupped bright pink, continuous.

'Pink Prosperity', 1931, Hybrid Musk, double mid-pink rosettes, scented, continuous.

'Pinkie', 1947, bush, semi-double rich pink, continuous.

—— 1947, climbing, semi-double rich pink, continuous.

'Pompon de Paris', 1839, China, small double pink rosettes, continuous.

'Popcorn', 1973, miniature, small semi-double creamy white, scented, continuous.

'Portland Rose', 1800, Portland, almost single bright pink, fragrant, recurrent.

'Poulsen's Park Rose', 1953, shrub, clusters, single soft clear pink, fragrant, recurrent.

'Président de Seze', 1836, Gallica, large very double lilac-pink, fragrant, spring.

'Pretty Jessica', 1983, English, shrub, very double rose-pink, very fragrant, continuous.

'Pride of Hurst', 1926, double salmon rosettes, continuous.

'Prosperity', 1919, Hybrid Musk, clusters, double pearly white, continuous.

'Prospero', 1982, English, shrub, very double rich red to purple, very fragrant, continuous.

'Proud Titania', 1982, English, shrub, large very double soft apricot, scented, recurrent.

'Queen Elizabeth', 1954, Floribunda, double pink, scented, continuous.

R. x alba, unknown, Alba, single white, fragrant, spring.

R. arvensis, rambler, single white with gold stamens, hips, fragrant, late spring.

R. banksiae alba plena, rambler, clusters, double white, violet scented, early spring.

R. banksiae lutea, rambler, clusters, double yellow, early spring.

R. banksiae lutescens, 1870, clusters, single yellow, early spring.

R. banksiae normalis, 1796, rambler, clusters, single white, evergreen, early spring.

R. bracteata, shrub/climber, single white with gold stamens, evergreen, fragrant, continuous.

R. brunonii, rambler, clusters, single white, very fragrant, late spring.

R. canina, shrub, single pink, hips, scented, late spring.

R. x cantabrigiensis, 1931, shrub, small single yellow, spring.

R. carolina, shrub, single rose-pink, fragrant, late spring.

R. centifolia, unknown, shrub, double dark pink, fragrant, spring.

R. chinensis, R. indica, shrub, single pink, continuous.

R. ciliata, shrub, single creamy white, hips, spring.

R. x damascena bifera, Autumn Damask, very ancient Damask, clusters, loosely double pale pink, very fragrant, continuous.

R. x dupontii, pre-1817, shrub, single white touched pink, hips, scented, spring.

R. eglanteria, R. rubiginosa, single mid-pink, hips, apple scent, spring.

R. farreri persetosa, shrub, small single pink, hips, spring.

R. fedtschenkoana, large shrub, single white.

R. filipes, rambler, clusters, single white, fragrant, late spring.

R. foetida, shrub, single yellow, perfumed, spring.

R. foetida bicolor, shrub, single orange with yellow reverse, perfumed, spring.

R. foetida persiana, shrub, double cupped yellow, perfumed, spring.

R. foliolosa, shrub, single pink, thornless, hips, fragrant, late spring.

R. fortuneana, c. 1845, rambler, large fully double milky white, scented, early spring.

R. gallica officinalis, ancient, Gallica (the Apothecary's Rose), single red, fragrant, late spring.

R. gentiliana, 1907, rambler, clusters, single white, hips,

scented, spring.

R. gigantea, rambler, large single pale yellow, hips, fragrant, recurrent.

R. glauca, *R. rubrifolia*, shrub, single pink, scented, late spring.

R. x *harisonii*, 1846, Scotch, double clear yellow, early spring.

R. helenae, rambler, clusters, single white, hips, fragrant, spring.

R. hugonis, 1899, shrub, single yellow, hips, early spring.

R. laevigata, rambler, single white, evergreen, fragrant, early spring.

R. longicuspis, pre-1915, climber, clusters, single white, evergreen, spring.

R. macrantha, shrub, single white, hips, scented, spring.

R. moschata, rambler, clusters, single white, scented, spring.

R. moschata nastarana, 'Persian Musk Rose', 1879, Hybrid Moschata, clusters, semi-double white, fragrant, spring.

R. moyesii, 1890, shrub, single soft rich red with gold stamens, hips, spring.

R. multiflora, rambler, clusters, single white, fragrant, spring.

R. nitida, small shrub, single rich red, hips, fragrant, late spring.

R. nutkana, 1876, shrub, single pale lavender-pink, hips, spring.

R. x *paulii*, 1900, Hybrid Rugosa, single white, spring.

R. pendulina, *R. alpina*, bush, single dark pink, hips, fragrant, late spring.

R. phoenicia, climber, large clusters, single white.

R. pimpinellifolia, *R. spinosissima*, small shrub, single whitish cream, hips, spring.

R. pimpinellifolia altaica, c. 1818, shrub, single white, hips, early spring.

R. roxburghii (plena), shrub, double mid-pink, chestnut-like hips, spring.

R. rugosa, shrub, single cerise-pink, hips, fragrant, recurrent.

R. rugosa alba, c. 1870, Rugosa, single white, hips, fragrant, continuous.

R. rugosa 'Typica', 1796, Rugosa, large single cerise-pink, hips, fragrant, recurrent.

R. sempervirens, rambler, single white, scented, spring.

R. sericea pteracantha, *R. omeiensis pteracantha*, single white, large red thorns, spring.

R. setigera, shrub/climber, single rose-pink, hips, fragrant, summer.

R. setipoda, shrub, large single pink, scented, spring.

R. stellata, 1902, dwarf shrub, single, violet-pink, spring.

R. sweginzowii, large shrub, single rich pink, hips, scented, spring.

R. villosa, *R. pomifera*, shrub, single pink, hips, scented, spring.

R. virginiana, small shrub, single pink, hips, scented, spring to summer.

R. virginiana plena, 'Rose d'Amour', pre-1870, shrub, double lilac-rose-pink, fragrant, recurrent.

R. webbiana, large shrub, single apricot-pink, hips, scented, late spring.

R. wichuraiana, 1860, rambler, single white, glossy evergreen, late spring.

'Radway Sunrise', 1962, shrub, single yellow to reddish tones, hips, continuous.

'Rambling Rector', unknown, Hybrid Multiflora Rambler, clusters, double white, scented, spring.

'Ramona', 1913, Hybrid Laevigata, single dark pink, light scent, recurrent.

'Raubritter', 1967, Hybrid Macrantha, cupped double silver-pink, scented, late spring.

'Red Coat', 1973, English, shrub, large almost single bright red, continuous.

'Reine des Violettes', 1860, Hybrid Perpetual, very double lilac-purple, scented, recurrent.

'Reine Marie Henriette', 1878, climbing Hybrid Tea, double violet-red, scented, continuous.

'René André', 1901, Wichuraiana Rambler, semi-double soft coral-apricot-pink, apple scented, semi-recurrent.

'Rêve d'Or', 1869, Noisette, double soft apricot, scented, recurrent.

'Ripples', 1971, Floribunda, double soft lavender-mauve, scented, continuous.

'Robin Hood', 1927, Hybrid Musk, clusters, single deep pink, scented, continuous.

'Roger Lambelin', 1890, Hybrid Perpetual, double maroon-red with white edges and markings, recurrent.

'Rosa Mundi', pre-1580, Gallica, single striped red and white, scented, spring.

'Rose de Meaux', pre-1789, Centifolia, small double soft pink rosettes, scented, spring.

'Rose de Rescht', unknown, Portland, very double lilac-red, fragrant, recurrent.

'Rose du Maître d'École', 1840, Gallica, very double mauvish pink, fragrant, spring.

'Rose du Roi à Fleurs Pourpres', 1819, Portland, very double reddish pink, fragrant, recurrent.

'Rose Marie Viaud', 1924, Hybrid Multiflora Rambler, clusters, very double purple, scented, late spring.

'Roseraie de l'Hay', 1901, Hybrid Rugosa, semi-double lilac-purple, very fragrant, recurrent.

'Rosette Delizy', 1922, Tea, very double yellow-pink, scented, continuous.

'Rouletii', 1922, miniature, small double rose-pink, continuous.

'Russelliana', 1840, Hybrid Multiflora, clusters, very double purple, very fragrant, spring.

'Sadler's Wells', 1983, Hybrid Musk, single white tinged red, scented, continuous.

'Safrano', 1839, Tea, double buff-yellow, scented, continuous.

'Sanders' White', 1912, Hybrid Wichuraiana, clusters, small white rosettes, recurrent.

'Sarah van Fleet', 1926, Hybrid Rugosa, double mid-pink, fragrant, recurrent.

'Scabrosa', unknown, Rugosa, single carmine-pink, hips, fragrant, recurrent.

'Scharlachglut', 'Scarlet Fire', 1952, Gallica, single bright red, hips, scented, spring.

'Schneezwerg', 1912, Hybrid Rugosa, small semi-double white with yellow stamens, hips, fragrant, continuous.

'Schoener's Nutkana', 1930, Hybrid Nutkana, single pink, fragrant, late spring.

'Sea Foam', 1964, rambler, clusters, loose double white

blushed pink, scented, continuous.

'Seagull', 1907, Hybrid Multiflora Rambler, semi-double white, fragrant, late spring.

'Sealing Wax', 1938 Hybrid Moyesii, single rich pink, hips, scented.

'Semi-plena', pre-1600, Alba, almost single white, early summer.

'Shot Silk', 1931, climbing Hybrid Tea, loose double rose-pink, fragrant, continuous.

'Shower of Gold', 1910, Hybrid Wichuraiana, large very double soft gold, scented, late spring.

'Silver Moon', 1931, Hybrid Laevigata, large almost single creamy white, late spring.

'Sir Clough', 1983, English, shrub, large lightly double cerise-pink, fragrant, continuous.

'Sir Frederick Ashton', 1985, Hybrid Tea, double creamy white, very fragrant, continuous.

'Slater's Crimson China', 1792, China, loose double dark red, continuous.

'Sneprincesse', 1946, Paree, cupped double white, continuous.

'Snow Carpet', 1980, ground-cover, small white rosettes, spring.

'Snowflake', 1866, Tea, double pure white, scented, continuous.

'Soleil d'Or', 1900, Hybrid Tea, very double apricot-yellow, fragrant, recurrent.

'Solfaterre', 1843, Noisette, large double soft sulphur-yellow, fragrant, continuous.

'Sombreuil', 1850, climbing Tea, very double creamy white blushed pink, very fragrant, recurrent.

'Sophie's Perpetual', rediscovered 1960, China, deep cerise-pink paling in the centre, fragrant, continuous.

'Souvenir de la Malmaison', 1843, Bourbon, very double soft powder-pink, very fragrant, continuous.

—— 1893, Climbing Bourbon, very fragrant, continuous.

'Souvenir de Mme Brieul', unknown, Bourbon, very double dark-pink, very fragrant, continuous.

'Souvenir de Mme Léonie Viennot', 1897, climbing Tea, loose double rose-pink with yellow base, scented, recurrent.

'Souvenir de Philomel Cochet', 1899, Hybrid Rugosa, very double white, fragrant, recurrent.

'Souvenir de St Anne's', 1950, Bourbon, almost single palest pink, very fragrant, continuous.

'Souvenir du Docteur Jamain', 1865, Hybrid Perpetual, double dark wine, fragrant, continuous.

'Souvenir d'un Ami', 1846, Tea, very double rose-pink, fragrant, continuous.

'Sparkler', 1929, Polyantha, clusters, small double red, continuous.

'Sparrieshoop', 1953, shrub/pillar, single warm pink, continuous.

'St. Nicholas', 1950, Damask, clusters, semi-double rose-pink, hips, spring.

'Stanwell Perpetual', 1838, Hybrid Pimpinellifolia, double soft pink, fragrant, continuous.

'Sutter's Gold', 1950, Hybrid Tea, double yellow with red flame, very fragrant, continuous.

—— 1950, climbing Hybrid Tea, double yellow with red flame, very fragrant, recurrent.

'Swany', 1978, procumbent shrub, clusters, double white, continuous.

'Tapis Volant', unknown, Hybrid Musk, single pink, continuous.

'Tausendschön', 1906, Hybrid Multiflora Rambler, double apricot-pink, light scent, spring.

'Tea Rambler', 1905, Hybrid Multiflora Rambler, double mid-pink, fragrant, continuous.

'The Bishop', unknown, Centifolia, very double cerise-pink, fragrant, spring.

'The Bride', 1885, Tea, semi-double white blushed pink, scented, continuous.

'The Fairy', 1932, Polyantha, clusters, small, double warm pink, continuous.

'The Garland', 1835, Hybrid Moschata, semi-double white, fragrant, spring.

'The Reeve', 1979, English, shrub, large globular warm pink, scented, continuous.

'The Squire', 1977, English, shrub, very double, dark red, very fragrant, continuous.

'Thisbe', 1918, Hybrid Musk, semi-double buff-white, scented, continuous.

'Thusnelda', 1886, Hybrid Rugosa, large double soft pink, fragrant, spring.

'Tinwell Moss', very old, Moss, very double bright pink, scented, spring.

'Tour de Malakoff', 1846, Centifolia, double lilac-purple, very fragrant, spring.

'Tricolore de Flandre', 1846, Gallica, double pink striped purple, scented, late spring.

'Trier', 1904, Hybrid Musk, clusters, small semi-double white, fragrant, recurrent.

'Trigintipetala', unknown, Damask, large loose double mid-pink, very fragrant, spring.

'Triomphe de Luxembourg', 1839, Tea, very double buff-pink, fragrant, continuous.

'Tuscany Superb', pre-1850, Gallica, double deep crimson, fragrant, spring.

'Uetersen', 1939, shrub/climber, clusters, fully double rich pink, recurrent.

'Ulrich Brunner Fils', 1882, Hybrid Perpetual, very double globular cerise-red, very fragrant, recurrent.

'Variegata di Bologna', 1909, Bourbon, double striped purple-pink-white, fragrant, recurrent.

'Vatertag', 1959, Paree, cupped double salmon-orange, continuous.

'Veilchenblau', 1909, Hybrid Multiflora Rambler, clusters, lightly double violet-purple, fragrant, late spring.

'Violette', 1921, Hybrid Multiflora Rambler, clusters, semi-double violet-purple, scented, late spring.

'Viridiflora', 1833, Chinensis, small double green rosettes, continuous.

'Wedding Day', 1851, Hybrid Sinowilsonii, clusters, single white with gold stamens, scented, late spring.

'Wenlock', 1984, English, shrub, large double purple-red, very fragrant, continuous.

'White Cécile Brunner', 1909, Chinensis, small double white, scented, continuous.

'White Duchesse de Brabant', 1909, Tea, loose-cupped double white, scented, continuous.

'White Flight', 1923, Hybrid Multiflora, semi-double white, scented, late spring.

'White Grootendorst', 1962, Hybrid Rugosa, clusters, double white, carnation style, continuous.

'White Sparrieshoop', 1962, shrub/pillar, clusters, single white, scented, continuous.

'White Wings', 1947, Hybrid Tea, large single satin-white, scented, continuous.

'Wife of Bath', 1969, English, shrub, double warm pink, scented, continuous.

'Wilhelm', 1944, Hybrid Musk, clusters, loose double wine-red, scented, continuous.

'William Allen Richardson', 1878, Noisette, clusters, soft apricot, scented, continuous.

'William Lobb', 1855, Moss, loose double purple-wine-red, fragrant, spring.

'William Shakespeare', 1987, English, shrub, very double deep crimson, fragrant, continuous.

'Windrush', 1984, English, shrub, large semi-double creamy yellow, hips, scented, continuous.

'Wintoniensis', 1928, Hybrid Moyesii, single deep pink, hips, scented, late spring.

'Wolly Dodd's Rose', pre-1790, hybrid species, semi-double warm pink, spring.

'Yellow Charles Austin', 1981, English, shrub/climber, very double yellow, fragrant, recurrent.

'Yesterday', 1974, shrub, clusters, small semi-double lavender-pink.

'York and Lancaster', *R.* x *damascena versicolor*, 1551, Damask, loosely double white-pink or variegated, fragrant, spring.

'Zenobia', 1899, Moss, large globular warm pink, very fragrant, spring.

'Zéphirine Drouhin', 1968, climbing Bourbon, double deep rose-pink, thornless, very fragrant, continuous.

Bibliography

Austin, David, *The Heritage of the Rose*, Antique Collectors' Club, U.K., 1988.

—— *Old Roses and English Roses*, Antique Collectors' Club, U.K., 1992.

Barker, Lady M.A., *Station Life in New Zealand*, Golden Press, Auckland, 1973, first published 1883.

Beales, Peter, *Classic Roses*, Collins Harvill, London, 1985.

—— *Twentieth-Century Roses*, Collins Harvill, London, 1988.

—— *Roses*, Harvill Harper Collins, London, 1992.

Beckett, Kenneth A., *The Concise Encyclopaedia of Garden Plants*, Orbis, London, 1978.

Bunyard, Edward A., *Old Garden Roses*, Earl M. Coleman, New York, 1978, first published 1936.

Coats, Peter, *Flowers in History*, Weidenfeld and Nicholson, London, 1970.

Curtis's Botanical Magazine, first published 1787.

Fairbrother, F., *Roses*, Penguin Books, Harmondsworth, Middlesex, 1958.

Fitter, Richard & Fitter, Alastair, *The Wild Flowers of Britain and Northern Europe*, Collins, London, 1974.

Genders, Roy, *Roses*, John Gifford, The Garden Book Club, London, 1959.

—— *The Rose: A Complete Handbook*, Robert Hale, London, 1965.

Gibson, Michael, *The Book of the Rose*, Macdonald General Books, London & Sydney, 1980.

Heritage Roses New Zealand, Journals of Heritage Roses New Zealand Inc., many and various.

Griffiths, Trevor, *My World of Old Roses*, vol 1, Whitcoulls, Christchurch, 1983.

—— *My World of Old Roses*, vol 2, Whitcoulls, Christchurch, 1986.

Harkness, Jack, *Roses*, J.M. Dent & Sons Ltd, London, 1978.

Harris, Cyril C., *The Rose Garden*, Ward Lock Ltd, London, 1974.

Hillier & Sons, *Hillier's Manual of Trees and Shrubs*, David & Charles, London, 1988.

Hobhouse, Penelope, *Colour in Your Garden*, Collins, London, 1985.

—— *Gertrude Jekyll on Gardening: An Anthology*, Macmillan, London, 1985.

Hortus, David Wheeler, Powys, many and various.

Itten, *The Elements of Colour*, Van Nostrand Reinhold, New York, 1970.

Jekyll, Gertrude, *Colour Schemes for the Flower Garden*, Frances Lincoln, London, 1987, first published 1914.

—— *The Gardener's Essential Gertrude Jekyll*, Robinson Publishing, London, 1991, first published 1964.

Keays, Ethelyn Emery, *Old Roses*, Earl M. Coleman, New York, 1978, first published 1935.

Keen, Mary, *Colour Your Garden*, Conran Octopus, London, 1991.

Kordes, Wilhelm, *Roses*, translated and edited by N.P. Harvey, Studio Vista, London, 1964.

Le Rougetel, Hazel, *A Heritage of Roses*, Unwin Hyman, London, 1988.

Mason, Alan & Mary, *Manual of Shrub and Old Roses*, Frank Mason & Son Ltd, Feilding, 4th ed., rev., 1985.

Mansfield, T.C., *Roses in Colour and Cultivation*, Collins, London, 1943, rev. ed. 1946.

New Zealand Gardener, New Zealand Gardener Publications, Auckland, many and various.

New Zealand Rose Annual, many and various.

Nottle, Trevor, *Growing Old-Fashioned Roses*, Kangaroo Press, Kenthurst, 1983.

—— *Old-Fashioned Gardens*, Godwit Press, Auckland, 1992.

Phillips, Roger & Rix, Martyn, *Roses*, Pan, U.K., 1988.

Polson, Gillian, *The Living Kitchen*, Benton Ross, Auckland, 1983.

Redgrove, Hugh (ed.), *A New Zealand Handbook of Bulbs and Perennials*, Godwit Press, Auckland, 1991.

Sackville-West, V., *The Illustrated Garden Book: A New Anthology* by Robin Lane Fox, Michael Joseph, London, 1986.

Schinz, Marina, *Visions of Paradise*, Thames and Hudson, London, 1985.

Shepherd, Roy E., *History of the Rose*, Earl M. Coleman, New York, 1978, first published 1954.

Steen, Nancy, *The Charm of Old Roses*, Reed Methuen, Auckland, 1987, first published 1966.

The Australian and New Zealand Rose Annual, various.

Thomas, A.S., *Better Roses*, Angus and Robertson, Sydney, 1950.

Thomas, Graham Stuart, *The Old Shrub Roses*, J.M. Dent & Sons Ltd, London, 1955.

—— *Shrub Roses of Today*, J.M. Dent & Sons Ltd, London, 1962.

—— *Climbing Roses Old and New*, J.M. Dent & Sons Ltd, London, 1965.

Verey, Rosemary, *Good Planting*, Frances Lincoln, London, 1990.

Index

Roses in the index without page references may be found in the annotated list beginning on page 170; all roses in the text are also summarised in this list. Italic type denotes photographs.